THE MYTH OF DEMOCRACY

TAGE LINDBOM was born in Sweden in 1909. He was once a dedicated socialist and one of the intellectual architects of the Swedish Welfare State. Having completed a doctorate in history at the University of Stockholm in 1938, he was for many years director of the Labor Movement Archives and Library, housed in the headquarters of the Swedish Labor Movement in Stockholm. Close to the very center of decision-making, Lindbom helped conceive and implement "the Swedish model." He was the friend of prime ministers, cabinet ministers, and labor leaders. He served on public boards and commissions dealing with cultural questions, including the executive board of the Royal Opera. After World War II Lindbom started to have serious doubts about the cause he had promoted. He underwent a slow but profound intellectual and spiritual change. In 1962 he published *The Windmills of Sancho Panza*, a book that rejected the assumptions behind Social Democracy and related movements. He found himself suddenly isolated. Since breaking with his past, Lindbom has published many books in Sweden, most of which explore the tension between religion and modern secular ideology. The present volume is the second of his books to appear in English. The first was *The Tares and the Good Grain* (1983).

CLAES G. RYN is professor of politics at The Catholic University of America. He has also taught at the University of Virginia. He is chairman of the National Humanities Institute and coeditor of *Humanitas*. Born and raised in Sweden, he has been widely published on both sides of the Atlantic. His books include *Democracy and the Ethical Life*; *Will, Imagination, and Reason*; and *The New Jacobinism: Can Democracy Survive?*

The Myth of Democracy

Tage Lindbom

with an introduction by

Claes G. Ryn

WILLIAM B. EERDMANS PUBLISHING COMPANY
GRAND RAPIDS, MICHIGAN / CAMBRIDGE U.K.

© 1996 Wm. B. Eerdmans Publishing Co.
255 Jefferson Ave. S.E., Grand Rapids, Michigan 49503
P.O. Box 163, Cambridge CB3 9PU U.K.

Printed in the United States of America

01 00 99 98 97 96   7 6 5 4 3 2 1

Library of Congress Cataloging-in-Publication Data

Lindbom, Tage, 1909-
[Selections. English. 1996]
The myth of democracy / Tage Lindbom.
p.   cm.
Contents: The myth of democracy — The ideology of
socialism — Lucifer.
ISBN 0-8028-4064-7 (alk. paper)
1. Democracy. 2. Socialism. 3. Social problems.
4. Church and social problems. I. Title.
JC423.L54213 1996
321.8 — dc20   96-5080
                                                      CIP

The title chapter, "The Myth of Democracy," is an English version of *Demokratin är en myt* (NORMA Bokförlag, Borås, Sweden, 1991), translated by the author, Tage Lindbom, and Alvin Moore, Jr., with assistance from Patrick A. Moore. "The Ideology of Socialism" was translated by Carl Johan Ljungberg. "Lucifer" was translated under the auspices of the Foundation for Traditional Studies and appeared in their *Religion of the Heart: Essays Presented to Frithjof Schuon,* 1991; it is used here courtesy of the Foundation. The whole has been revised and edited by Alvin Moore, Jr., and Claes G. Ryn has contributed an introduction.

Contents

To the memory of

Russell Kirk

Introduction

CLAES G. RYN

Western intellectuals and politicians, especially in the United States, are writing and speaking about the triumphs and salvific powers of Western democracy. Democracy is the destiny of humanity, they proclaim. All peoples of the world yearn for it, and those who enjoy its blessings have the obligation of bringing it to others as soon as possible. The fall of Soviet communism has seemed to validate democratist triumphalism. Yet there is a widening gap between democratist rhetoric and concrete reality. Democratism is surging in the midst of deepening social and political problems in the Western world. These include precipitously falling standards of personal and public conduct, declining education, spreading political opportunism, demagoguery and corruption, social and political fragmentation, destruction of the family, rampant sexual promiscuity, drug use, and crime. Western man is displaying self-indulgence and irresponsibility on a scale that earlier generations would have deemed incompatible with liberty under law. As most individuals devote themselves to personal pleasures and creature comforts, political leaders and intellectuals contemplate ever new roles for government. Elections are increasingly empty rituals legitimating the exercise of central power. The unceasing praise for democracy looks like an escape from troublesome reality, but it also dresses up a cynical drive for power.

The problems of Western society are sufficiently severe to raise doubts about democracy's ability to survive. Understanding the present situation requires not mainly specialized studies but a better grasp of the origins of problems and the connections between them. Large questions suggest themselves. For instance, is the deterioration of Western democracy due to factors extraneous to that form of government? Or is democracy, by its very nature, doomed to deteriorate in some such manner as is now occurring in the Western world? The Austrian thinker Erik von Kühnelt-Leddihn, for example, argues that the main problems of democracy are *systembedingt,* that is, inherent in popular government itself: Majority rule must lead to lowered political standards and a general erosion of civilization.

According to the Swedish historian and philosopher-theologian Tage Lindbom, one can fully understand democracy only in its spiritual significance. The emergence and entrenchment of democracy in the Western world, he argues, forms part of a historical development whose central meaning is an attempt to deny the sovereignty of God. The notion of popular sovereignty expresses and advances a process of secularization with important origins already in medieval times. The "great constitutional question," Lindbom writes in *The Myth of Democracy,* is "Who will rule, God or man?" Contemporary Western democracy and egalitarianism represent the culmination of the effort to establish the Kingdom of Man.

Rebel in the Welfare State

Defenders of democracy and equality cannot dismiss Lindbom as a mere outsider who does not understand the moral power of these modern goals. Lindbom is intimately familiar with their appeal. Well into his mature years he lived and promoted the democratic-egalitarian dream himself. Now in his eighties, he was once an intellectual leader of Swedish Social Democracy. He was one of the architects of the social model that would so fascinate "progressives" around the world. Lindbom knew well the leaders of the Social Democratic governments that constructed the Swedish Welfare State. Having written his doctoral dissertation on the labor union movement in Sweden, he was appointed director of the Labor Movement Archives and Library in Stockholm. He also served on public boards and commissions dealing with cultural questions.

As the Swedish Social Democrats expanded the Welfare State after World War II, real and sustained dissent became increasingly rare. Socialists and nonsocialists criticized each other and competed in very close elections, but the initiative lay with the proponents of further expansion of the responsibilities of government. A far-reaching consensus emerged that blurred the line between socialists and nonsocialists. Such was the strength of the new orthodoxy that more than marginal deviation would place a career in jeopardy. Even those who criticized the Social Democrats usually assumed that the Swedish way, or something like it, was the way of the future. Applause from abroad, not least from American intellectuals and journalists, seemed to confirm this view. A prominent Swedish liberal professor of political science, Herbert Tingsten, who had become editor-in-chief of the country's most influential newspaper, proclaimed the death of ideology. Welfare state democracy had so clearly demonstrated its superiority, he argued, that ideological conflict was now bound to peter out. If Tingsten's argument sounds familiar, it is because it had American antecedents and has reappeared in the United States three decades later under the heading "The End of History."

It took many years before Tage Lindbom's doubts about the cause he was advancing evolved into a coherent new outlook and before he made his deepest criticisms public. In 1962 the prestige of the Swedish Welfare State was still rising. It was then that Lindbom published the book that would once and for all sever his connection with the movement to which he had devoted his life. *The Windmills of Sancho Panza* was in every respect offensive to Swedish orthodoxy. It challenged the very foundations of the system that was heralded as the ultimate of social and political enlightenment. Lindbom criticized the dearest of all of its goals — equality. He rejected the notion of the People as the source of all authority. He traced the historical origins of these beliefs and rejected them as inimical to the natural order and as the products of an almost childlike imagination. To take more shame on himself in secularized Sweden, Lindbom contended that there can be no brotherhood of man without the fatherhood of God.

Lindbom's days as a respected and influential author were over. Still in his mid-fifties, he retired from his library directorship. A small pension and his wife's income as a psychotherapist enabled him to devote more time to reading and reflection. But no longer could he count on outlets for his writing. He managed to place his books, if sometimes with great difficulty, but they were almost completely ignored in mainstream newspapers and journals. Some of his work appeared in French and German translation.

I am well familiar with the Swedish situation; I was born in Sweden, grew up and received most of my education there. I graduated from the Gymnasium in my home city the year after the publication of *The Windmills of Sancho Panza*. It is relevant that I received a graduation award, primarily, I believe, for work in philosophy. The award was accompanied by a book of which I had never heard — *The Windmills of Sancho Panza*.

4

Since the book was not widely known and had an unusual thesis, the award committee, or a member of it, had obviously thought that it would hold special interest for me. So it did. I read the book with sympathy and admiration, although not without reservations. It helped to articulate my dissent from the ethical, intellectual, and cultural direction of my country.

A few years later I would get to know the author. Tage Lindbom is a man of medium height and build with a slight stoop and a bald head. His manner is gracious and kindly. His pensive demeanor and veiled, inwardly gaze are those of one given to deep reflection. Yet his conversation is not ethereal or abstract but often concrete, lively, and amusing. His stories about the personalities and foibles of old acquaintances who were prime minsters, cabinet members, or labor leaders are told with humor and vividness.

I too was headed for trouble with the Swedish consensus. At the universities positivism stifled humanistic-scholarly inquiry into such subjects as the ethical dimension and preconditions of culture and of social and political order. While at Uppsala University I founded a national intellectual organization dedicated to philosophical renewal. Tage Lindbom offered his strong support. My own questioning of the reigning academic orthodoxy and related sociopolitical and cultural phenomena was framed in philosophical rather than religious terms, but it ran parallel in important respects to Lindbom's. My chances for an academic career in Sweden dwindled.

Democracy and Secularization

Most of Lindbom's work since the publication of *The Windmills of Sancho Panza* has expanded on the themes of that book. In a series of small volumes he has examined the basic assump-

tions of major political, intellectual, and cultural currents of
the last two hundred years. He has given much attention to
the modern ideologies, particularly to socialism and Marxism.
His central concern has been what ideas and phenomena say
about man's relationship to God. Lindbom's writing is predom-
inantly philosophical and historical, but it erases the line between philosophy and theology. Sometimes it takes on the tenor
of a spiritual meditation.

Prior to the present volume only one other book by Lindbom was available in English translation, *The Tares and the Good
Grain* (Mercer University Press, 1983). It too is representative
of his general position and method. It argues that the altruis-
tic-sounding slogans and exhortations of the modern ideologies
conceal either individual or collective selfishness. It did not
take long in the evolution of modernity for the early stress on
liberty to yield to greed and the desire for power. Today's attacks
on traditional society, religious symbols, the family, parental
authority, the differences between the sexes, and inequality are
for Lindbom the final stages of an attempt to overturn the
created order. As Western man proclaims his autonomy from
God, he moves not toward self-fulfillment but toward degradation, even a loss of identity. Fatherless, he descends into an
infantile, morally chaotic existence.

In *The Myth of Democracy* Lindbom analyzes some of the
most important elements of the protracted process that finally
produced the modern myth of self-governing Man. From the
beginning of Jewish-Christian civilization it is possible to observe
a secularizing dynamic involving dialogue between God and
man, "between the heavenly and the earthly, between the spiritual and the sensory orders, between the intellective and the
rational." What soils and subverts the created order is mankind's
rebelliousness, which denies the "hierarchical and the celestial"
and tries to subordinate the terrestrial to human power.

In Lindbom's view, the secularizing impulse received an important boost with the introduction of Aristotelian natural philosophy and logic into Christianity. Other efforts to establish earthly knowledge independent of the knowledge of God had the same effect. The most important advance for secularization in the medieval period, Lindbom argues, was initiated by William of Ockham, who separated faith and knowledge. The experimentalist understanding of nature pushed God further away from creation. By the time of the Enlightenment the outlines for a coming spiritual disaster were discernible. Increasingly, the destructive work was done by the twin forces of rationalism and sensualism. They are, Lindbom writes, "the two forms of consciousness whereby secularization floods the Western world." Not only does secularization undermine a hierarchical view of the world and society and prepare the way for egalitarianism; it unleashes humanity's vegetative desires. Lying at the end of this development, democracy becomes the servant of those desires. Among the modern secularizing influences to which Lindbom gives particular attention are Jean-Jacques Rousseau, the French Revolution, liberalism, Marxism, socialism, Heidegger, and cybernetics.

As the democratic-egalitarian forces extend their dominion, they produce human beings sunk more and more deeply in a vegetative state. Despite all the proud talk of self-rule and noble citizenship, democratic men are really political subjects. They are increasingly passive, lonely wards of an expanding and busily administrating superstate, a modern Leviathan.

The gathering signs of social and cultural disintegration have for Lindbom a profoundly disturbing spiritual significance. They disclose a "Luciferian process." Every traditional religious and higher human aspiration is being denied. Cruelty and perversity are flourishing. In the arts, "the ugly, the distorted, the morbid, the malicious are mobilized." "Secularized man proclaims himself as light bearer; instead he is prisoner of the Lord of Darkness." Modern democracy and equality reveal their true nature as a denial of divine authority. Far from creating harmony and peace of mind, they produce disharmony and anxiety. Neurosis has become a mass phenomenon. A sense of guilt is spreading from which man cannot escape in spite of his restless pursuit of sensual gratification. The guilt points to the ultimate source of his distress: pride — *superbia* — the first and greatest of the seven deadly sins. Postmodern Western man is facing a desperate situation marked by "Luciferian confusion." But, writes Lindbom, "every day man can meet God."

Intellectual Affinities and Parallels

Lindbom's work owes much of its distinctiveness to his intimate, more than intellectual familiarity with the modern ideological myths. His growing doubts about them were not merely theoretical but deeply personal. Lindbom's move away from socialism involved a spiritual transformation. It was accompanied and structured by much reading. Writers who influenced his change of heart or later affected his thinking include Titus Burckhardt, Ananda Coomaraswamy, René Guénon, Martin Lings, and especially Frithjof Schuon, author of such works as *The Transcendent Unity of Religions* and *Light on the Ancient Worlds*.

Although Lindbom seems to have been little influenced by them, he has much in common with thinkers well known in the United States who have dissented from dominant intellectual opinion. He resembles Eric Voegelin, for example, in his view of ideology, his treatment of religious symbols and myths, his belief that humans exist "between heaven and earth" (the title of one of Lindbom's books), and his Platonizing, ecumenical approach to religion. Lindbom's central theme, man trying to take God's place, has been a recurring motif also in the work of such writers as Thomas Molnar and Gerhart Niemeyer. His anti-egalitarian and anti-majoritarian ideas call to mind Erik von Kühnelt-Leddihn. His view of Rousseau and of the interplay of Baconian science and utopian-sentimental dreaming could have been derived from Irving Babbitt. Lindbom's belief that Western theology and philosophy took a disastrous turn with William of Ockham reminds one, for example, of Richard Weaver's indictment of Ockham and nominalism in *Ideas Have Consequences* (1948).[1] Citing *The Tares and the Good Grain,* Russell Kirk warmly endorsed Lindbom in the seventh edition of *The Conservative Mind* (1986).[2]

The egalitarian welfare state based on the Swedish model, which long has held such fascination for American "liberals," has lost its lustre in Sweden. The moral, cultural, intellectual, political, and economic consequences of what the American journalist Marquis Childs praised in 1938 as "the third way" have been widely bemoaned in Sweden for years.[3] Even leading Social Democrats have conceded the illusory nature of some of their old beliefs. Repairing the damage is proving difficult,

1. Of the many books by authors mentioned in this paragraph that could be cited as offering parallels to Lindbom's thinking, the following list is merely suggestive: Eric Voegelin, *From Enlightenment to Revolution* (Durham: Duke University Press, 1975); Thomas Molnar, *Utopia, the Perennial Heresy* (New York: Sheed and Ward, 1967); Gerhart Niemeyer, *Between Nothingness and Paradise* (Baton Rouge: Louisiana State University Press, 1971); Erik von Kühnelt-Leddihn, *Liberty or Equality?* (Caldwell: Caxton Printers, 1952); Irving Babbitt, *Literature and the American College* (Washington, D.C.: National Humanities Institute, 1986 [1908]); Richard Weaver, *Ideas Have Consequences* (Chicago: University of Chicago Press, 1965 [1948]).

2. Russell Kirk, *The Conservative Mind,* 7th rev. ed. (Chicago and Washington, D.C.: Regnery Books, 1986), vi-vii.

3. Marquis Childs, *Sweden: The Middle Way,* rev. ed. (New Haven: Yale University Press, 1961 [1938]).

however, partly because of confusion about the sources of the problems. In the United States there is some residual deep suspicion of intrusive government, and religion is still a notable influence. For these reasons, and despite the old American fondness for equality, perhaps many Americans will be more receptive to Lindbom's warnings than were his fellow Swedes. Because it is based on a reconstructed theocentric worldview, *The Myth of Democracy* will presumably appeal most to religious readers, but as one who has worked his way out of shattered modern illusions, Lindbom should also interest others who now face a disillusionment similar to his. At minimum, his forthright and courageous dissent from dominant Western opinion will balance smug appraisals of the state of Western society.

Some Reflections

This is not the place to attempt a rounded assessment of Lindbom's work. As a way of further elucidating his position, it may be helpful, however, to indicate the kind of questions and reservations that might be advanced, not by hostile critics but by sympathetic readers willing to ponder his ideas.

Lindbom's work draws on great philosophical and historical learning. Yet religious intuition orients his reasoning. He will sometimes bypass seemingly important philosophical distinctions and complications in order to formulate what is to him the heart of a matter. It might be argued in support of his philosophical-theological method that, since his reasoning is informed by a spiritual vision, a reader who is not attuned to that vision will not be persuaded by his argument in any case. It is true that Lindbom has little chance of reaching committed atheists or rigid positivists; to them, his point of view is simply "unscientific." But it may be different with genuine seekers who think of themselves as irreligious or as not traditionally religious. They will be more receptive to evidence regarding ethical-spiritual reality if it is not presented as inseparable from a particular religious point of view.

Here it is relevant that the ethical life and even transcendence have an experiential basis that is not dependent on dogmatic and revealed religion but can be elaborated philosophically. Philosophical inquiry in the last two centuries into the immanent, historical dimension of the divine and the universal has not simply served the divinization of humanity that so bothers Lindbom. Deepened and broadened interest in what falls within man's historical existence has furthered a more concrete, experiential understanding of spiritual reality. Lindbom himself often speaks of the human consciousness as participating in the divine, but his view of the modern world as dethroning God disinclines him to look within modernity as such for sources of new religious and ethical insight. He also has a strong Platonic inclination to separate the highest reality from the concrete, phenomenal world in which we live.

One may agree that modernity has produced great amounts of questionable and even perverse speculation and sentiment and still recognize that it also contains much that is fruitful. There are nonrationalistic and nonpositivistic modern sources that, though partly polluted, have provided important new ideas for ethics, theology, epistemology, and aesthetics. Of the important advances brought by modernity one might mention the historical sense, the discovery of the possible synthesis of universality and individuality, and the discovery of the creativity of the imagination. To the extent that Lindbom touches on these elements of thought, he tends to reduce them to his accustomed terms of secularization and divinization.

Lindbom sometimes appears to believe that the Western

world has deteriorated so far that those who seek to maintain their spiritual and intellectual integrity can do little except enter the catacombs, as it were. Those who would keep the spiritual flame alive in these worsening circumstances must not be discouraged, however, but should be diligent in resisting the pressures of the world. Lindbom himself has worked tirelessly at his own writing. *Ora et labora.* He sees efforts of this kind as necessary to spiritual health in the present, but they may one day also assist people who must start anew in the ruins of the old.

Like others who have put forth a religiously inspired critique of modernity — Voegelin, for instance — Lindbom assumes that only a spiritual awakening could redeem Western society. Yet he does not inquire into what specific forms such a revival might take or into what should be done practically in the meantime. Although Lindbom's work contains many realistic, perspicacious observations about present conditions, his thinking does not easily lend itself to formulating or assessing concrete possibilities for action. His criticism of modernity and his invocation of God make a certain spiritual attitude seem more important than exploring how, concretely, one could address the troubles of the here and now. To Lindbom's Platonizing theological mind, strong interest in actual historical opportunities offered by a highly imperfect world may betray an insufficiently spiritual attitude. Perhaps there is even an element of continuity between his reluctance to consider practical possibilities and his old socialist-utopian discomfort with the world as it is.

The reader of *The Myth of Democracy* is asked to consider the possibility that democracy is quintessentially the manifestation of a spiritual debacle, the enactment of the Kingdom of Man. In one limited way, Lindbom resembles those who extol democracy as the future of the world. Like them, he is not prone

12

to ask whether popularly oriented governments might appear in qualitatively different forms. He sees democracy, whatever its shape, as evolving in a particular, seemingly fated direction. If there are differences between particular popular governments, those differences are less important in the long run than is the historical dynamic that democracies have in common.

Can any form of government then be inherently just one thing and not another? Do not all actual governments mix different elements, so that, in concrete practice, as distinguished from abstract theory, they are complex constellations of partly conflicting forces? For example, all governments — even harsh dictatorships — must be "democratic" in the limited sense that to be functional they must have at least the grudging acceptance of the population. As for democracies, including the most egalitarian and majoritarian, they have to be at the same time "oligarchic" in that a people cannot rule itself *en masse:* it must have leaders. Lindbom makes the latter point himself, but he does not take up a larger discussion of the varied potentialities of democracy.

In my opinion it is essential to distinguish between majoritarian, plebiscitary democracy, on the one hand, and constitutional, representative popular rule on the other. These, I have argued, are not really different versions of one and the same type of government but are constituted by wholly different views of human nature and society and by wholly different institutions. Elements of these opposed forms often coexist in particular societies, but they are mutually destructive and ultimately incompatible.[4]

4. The distinction between plebiscitary and constitutional popular rule is developed at length in Claes G. Ryn, *Democracy and the Ethical Life,* expanded ed. (Washington, D.C.: The Catholic University of America Press, 1990 [LSU Press, 1978]); see also Ryn, *The New Jacobinism: Can Democracy Survive?* (Washington, D.C.: National Humanities Institute, 1991).

Plebiscitary democracy tries to conform government policy to the wishes of the majority. It assumes that the great mass of people are the best judges of their own interests and that they are even possessed of goodness, as proclaimed by Jean-Jacques Rousseau. Public officials should not make laws and decisions in a spirit of independence but be agents of current popular opinion. Vesting ultimate authority in the majority, plebiscitary democracy tends to expand and to centralize government and to politicize all social existence. Whatever the theory of majoritarianism, in practice it means that politicians cater to the lowest common denominator of popular opinion. Society is subjected to often short-sighted, superficial, and purely partisan wishes.

Constitutional popular government involves self-imposed restraints and representative arrangements. The framers of the U.S. Constitution intended a government based in general on popular consent, but the term "democracy" carried for them distasteful connotations: demagoguery, rabble-rousing, popular irresponsibility, and the like. These were serious dangers to be protected against. The framers had no interest in empowering a numerical national majority. That would have meant disregarding the corporate interests of states and other political subdivisions and dissolving the American people into an undifferentiated mass of individuals. The framers did not assume that all should carry the same weight in elections, as demanded by the majoritarian formula "one-man-one-vote." They envisioned wide but not universal suffrage. They also incorporated aristocratic or quasi-aristocratic features into popularly oriented rule. Such institutions as the Senate, the Supreme Court, and the presidency were to be filled by highly qualified individuals capable of articulating the long-term interests of the people independently of the popular pressures of the moment. Elected and non-elected officials were expected to follow their own conscience and best understanding, but also — in keeping with the framers' distrust of human nature — to have restricted powers. It was assumed that the national government as a whole would be limited, much power being retained by state and local governments, and that most of social life would be left to the discretion of individuals and groups in their private capacities.

Constitutional popular rule places heavy burdens on the citizens. It may be the most demanding form of government. In the absence of high degrees of responsibility and foresight in both voters and public officials, constitutional democracy begins to destroy itself. Because of the moral, intellectual, and cultural prerequisites of constitutional popular rule, it is not a realistic possibility in many countries. Partly for that reason, advocates of spreading democracy around the world are not prone to pursue a distinction between constitutional and plebiscitary democracy.

Democracy, in sum, does not have any single distinctive form or essence. It does have certain potentialities that, if permitted to develop, undermine not only all higher human aspirations but popular rule itself. In a very different form and in generally favorable circumstances, popularly oriented government need not be incompatible with civilized standards.

The possibility of constitutional democracy, as here defined, would appear to present a complication for Lindbom's reasoning. This form of government shows the influence of the old Western classical and Christian traditions, including their understanding of human nature and the purpose of society. Constitutional democracy implies respect for ethical universality in some form. Most of those who framed the American Constitution were men of Christian faith. Plebiscitary democracy, by contrast, springs almost exclusively from modern thought and sentiment of a particular kind. It has important sources in the egalitarian and

15

romantic ideas of Jean-Jacques Rousseau, which Lindbom discusses at length in *The Myth of Democracy*.

Is this a distinction without a difference? Lindbom probably would not say that it is, were he to reflect on the matter. But having concluded that the modern world has been moving inexorably toward secularization, he is not predisposed to take up considerations of this kind. All of Western democracy impresses him as dominated, more or less, by a spiritually insidious egalitarian momentum. Popular sovereignty, which can be shown to have a wide range of possible meanings, strikes him as being essentially an expression of the wish to dethrone God. Yet Lindbom's specific descriptions of democracy fit well only what has here been called plebiscitary, majoritarian democracy.

Granted that Western societies have evolved in such a way as to erode the chances for constitutional democracy, was the latter doomed to failure from the start because of concessions to popular consent? An alternative view is that history does not move inexorably but always presents opportunities for developing given circumstances in different, perhaps unexpected directions. What looks in hindsight like an overwhelming historical force with a definite direction is in fact the accumulation of individual human choices made at particular times. To assume that democracy has a single essence seems to discount the opposed potentialities of life.

If Alexis de Tocqueville was right that a democratic era had dawned in the Western world, what was the proper course of action for those who recognized the dangers of popular rule? Was it to stand rigidly athwart the building current until they were overwhelmed by it? Or was it to try, from the very beginning, to give the current the most civilized direction possible? The fact that the old American quasi-aristocratic constitutional order is today succumbing to majoritarian and egalitarian trends does not prove that it had to fail because of its element of popular consent. Given the historical situation, what other form of government would have been preferable? Would absolute monarchy, say, even have been a realistic possibility? At least in America, constitutional, representative popular rule may have had the best chance of averting the danger of plebiscitary democracy.

One should not assume that Tage Lindbom would simply reject these arguments, but he does leave the impression that once the secularizing forces had advanced beyond a certain point, their momentum became well-nigh irresistible. Whether this was the case is one of the provocative questions posed by *The Myth of Democracy*. The book turns the tables on our progressivist age. The forces of smugness will resent and dismiss Lindbom's perspective. Less sanguine readers may be bothered by it, but they will perhaps also be challenged to rethink some of their basic assumptions. Agree or disagree with Lindbom's religious intuition and philosophical inferences, they counter the modern tendency to facile, wishful thinking. He incisively confronts dimensions of problems with which Western intellectuals are increasingly unable or unwilling to deal but which require close attention.

Tage Lindbom addresses questions that hardly permit of definitive answers. People of religious, moral, and philosophical sensibility will differ among themselves about such questions, but they will share a sense of urgency and foreboding and disagree in a spirit of humility.

The Myth of Democracy

The owl of Minerva flies at nightfall.

HEGEL

Who will rule, God or man? This is the great constitutional question of human existence; this is the question that determines everything in mortal life, and especially and most acutely our social arrangements. Times of faith give way to times of unbelief; times of obedience, harmony, and resemblance to our prototype are replaced by times of disobedience, rebellion, and denial. The perennial question is always whether we humans are to understand our presence on this earth as a vice-regency or trusteeship under the mandate of heaven and the divine commandments, or whether we must strive to emancipate ourselves from any higher dominion, with human supremacy as our ultimate aim.

This conflict is already evoked in the Fall. The Serpent's promise to primordial Man has a twofold content. By eating of the fruit of the tree of the knowledge of good and evil, and thereby defying the divine command, Man will emancipate himself from dependence on heaven and will at the same time win the promise to become "like God," knowing good and evil. With this dual content of the Fall — to be free of our contingent nature, which is ineluctably dependent on heaven, and to become "equal" by gaining a knowledge that belongs solely to the Divine — we can perceive the contours of the City of Man.

18

These two fundamental ideological "archetypes," liberty and equality, are now formulated and expressed. But the Fall also has a double content in a purely cognitive sense: the tree of knowledge attracts not only by yielding enhanced mental capacity; its succulent fruit also gives sensual pleasure. The Fall thereby links two central powers of the human nervous system, the cerebral and the instinctive.

These two ideological prototypes, like the two faculties of rationalism and sensualism, indicate the essential elements in the process that we call secularization, a process having the earthly and the horizontal, the one-dimensional, as lodestar; as a consequence, they comprise a tendency to deny the hierarchical and the celestial. Secularization also brings with it progressive terrestrial conquests that have as their aim the enhancement of human power. We therefore add to the two prototypes, liberty and equality, a third element: terrestrial power.

In Judeo-Christian civilization it is possible to regard the process of secularization as a continuous dialogue between the heavenly and the earthly, between the spiritual and the sensory orders, between the intellective and the rational. It is always possible for the City of Man to challenge and defy the City of God by scientific and technological progress and achievement. The Old Testament tells of the Tower of Babel, and presents the art of brickmaking as an important technological means for the realization of chimerical enterprises. The Scriptures tell of the spiritual consequences.

In the history of the modern West, secularization gains its first foothold in the high Middle Ages when Aristotelian logic and natural philosophy intrude into the Western worldview. An important step in this direction occurs in the thirteenth century when the English Franciscan monk Roger Bacon affirms that mathematics is a method whereby human thinking can establish mundane, objective truth. As Prometheus had stolen fire from the gods and thereby threatened to bring about equality between heaven and earth, just so through mathematics it will become possible to gain a knowledge that is equal to divine truth.

In the next century there is an even more premonitory irruption into medieval Christianity: the nominalism of William of Ockham. Ockham delivers a telling blow against the conception of creation as a total unity, a macrocosm, by proclaiming that existence is a *multiversum:* that everything is individual, discrete, atomic, and separate from all else. Even God is not exempt from all of this; even he is *una res,* a thing among other things; and this means that God is separated from his creation. We humans experience the world through our sensory and mental faculties; and we believe that the resulting concepts, derived from sense data, provide us with real knowledge. And, Ockham adds, as God is not present in the world, we can have no real knowledge of him. We can only believe.

This represents a fundamental upheaval, a veritable revolution in medieval thinking. It is against this background that we must understand Martin Luther's *sola fide,* by belief alone. Only an ardent creed can overcome the void that Ockham has introduced between heaven and earth. For Ockham, the real is what our senses perceive. For traditional man, on the contrary, reality is a translucent objectivity, perceptible through the world of sensory experience; natural things are lamps through which shines the light of their heavenly — ultimately Divine — prototypes. But Ockham replaces this with a misplaced subjectivity, the consciousness that we gain through our sensory and mental faculties. The real is the evidence of the senses. Ockhamism informs "truth" or reality with a new content: it is this-worldly, subjective, gained by mental processes, especially rational and logical processes that depend on sense data.

First the Renaissance, then humanism, then the baroque:

here is the schema of a more and more profane conception of existence, an increasingly secularized world. Science, technology, aesthetics, social and political power — all of these become more and more the dominating elements in the consciousness of Western man. To be sure, all changes — most of which can be regarded as progress — can be considered in some manner as honoring God, as *ad majorem Dei gloriam;* but the baroque state brings with it a wholly mundane notion of monarchical sovereignty; it downgrades medieval unity and its theocentric conception of power. Rational thinking becomes more and more the guide for worldly activity, and this tendency finds its philosophical perfection in the French thinker and mathematician René Descartes, who, in 1637, publishes his famous *Discours de la Méthode.*

Just as Ockham's aim is to enlighten, to raise the level of intelligence, to inculcate proper thinking (*ad exercitanda ingenia),* so Descartes arrives at his "pure thought." Descartes, like Ockham, looks out on the landscape of natural science and regards the inquiring human mind, *res cogitans,* as the subject, while the object is the world of things, *res extensa,* whatever "takes up space." Like Ockham, he separates the credal world from the world of positive science, the road of science being that of "methodical doubt." And at last he states his great philosophical achievement: Space and matter are declared to be one.

Ratio, reason, working through the vertebral nervous system, now has its fully developed profane philosophical demarcation; and *Discours de la Méthode* is the fundamental document of modern scientific positivism. But man also has a passive and involuntary component in his complex nature; and this is where he confronts pleasure, sensual enjoyment. Sensualism is brought to its philosophical perfection when, in 1690, the English thinker John Locke publishes his *Essay Concerning*

Human Understanding. Locke does not deny that a higher Being may exist and consequently that a wisdom anterior to reason may also exist; but according to him, we live on the earth with our sensory endowments and we must adhere to this condition. Life is like a passage between Scylla and Charybdis, pleasure and pain. Man wishes and tries to avoid suffering; therefore life must be a calculation, with sensory delight as its guiding star. Pragmatically and empirically, we must try to find our way through life by continual trial and error. Man must learn to plan and to contrive, and thereby sensualism acquires a social aim: fear and suffering must be eliminated, not only from individual life but also from the life of society. We can see the outlines of the modern welfare state prefigured in all of this.

We might say, without undue simplification or distortion, that secularization increasingly becomes identified with two motives: the reduction of human intelligence to rationalism, and sensual desire; the one is grafted onto the vertebral nervous system, and the other is a function of the involuntary and subconscious elements of man's composite nature. Rationalism and sensualism will prove to be the mental currents and the two forms of consciousness whereby secularization floods the Western world. Human pride, *superbia,* the first and greatest of the seven deadly sins, grows unceasingly; and it is during the eighteenth century that man begins to formulate the notion that he is discovering himself as the earthly agent of power. Striving to exalt himself, he begins to doubt and deny what thousands of years of wisdom have faithfully held: that creation as we know it is enclosed within the formal order, and that being bound to forms it is intrinsically contradictory and imperfect. Yet man begins to believe that he lives in a world without confines and that there are no limits to human power. In this growing narcissism, Man and Mankind appear as an abstract set of twins.

The entire Western establishment, constituted through the labor of countless centuries, even millennia, and correlated with countless traditional ideas of value and principles of order, will in the eighteenth century be placed in doubt. First of all, doubt begins to erode the belief that we live under a heavenly Father who is both Creator and Legislator. The times are now propitious for a revolutionary change of scene.

II

The French Revolution of 1789 has one preeminent content: condemning the old traditional order, it proclaims a new structuring of human life. When I use the terms *traditionalism* and *modernism,* I am aware that I am using words and concepts. Both of these terms have many nuances and both can be interpreted in many ways; but they nevertheless express two different conceptions of life and consciousness. Traditionalism is founded, first of all, on the consciousness of a higher, divine Reality, an immutable power determining terrestrial and sensory actuality. Existence in all of its multiform and inconstant variety is nevertheless a unity that includes all of the innumerable individualities that exist in time and space; it is an equilibrium that is neither chance, accident, nor chaos. Spiritual power dominates creation, and man is therefore subject to spiritual as well as to social modalities of being and acting; he is subject to both a spiritual and a social order. Every human being carries within his heart, at the inmost center of his individual existence, a spiritual and immortal kernel. Man is a creature of cosmic proportions; not in any hubristic sense, but rather in the sense that he lives in community vertically as well as horizontally. Traditional man has the capacity for an objective conception of

23

Being because in his heart he is conscious of immortal and objective Reality.

Modernism denies the traditional, first because it desires a "free hand" to engage in continuous change, which is usually linked with the notion of everlasting progress — a "development" that allegedly leads always to higher and higher levels. Hierarchy, authority, tradition extended in duration, and norms extended through society — all of these are regarded by the modernist as so many obstacles to historical dynamism and relativism. For the modernist, history is the story of rapid change in which all things are relative; and these he considers as permanently necessary conditions, necessary in order to open new and expanding fields for human activity. Instead of the immutably objective there must be substituted a subjectivism that elevates Man to the position of central Power in his own conception of existence. Modernism replaces a perennial cosmic equilibrium with an atomistic "liberty" in a world conceived sometimes as a vacuum, sometimes as a field of exploitation for human conquest.

Growing secularization has as its converse a continuous weakening of traditional values. The image of God in man is unremittingly attenuated, its contours progressively blurred. The role of the Divine in terrestrial operations and events is steadily diminished, at least in man's consciousness; more and more he comes to think that he and he alone is sovereign on the earth. Finally, the power that dominates the world changes hands; heaven and earth are now like separate continents. But even this does not yet mean that heaven must be denied. It means rather that earthly interests and activities now dominate men's lives and thinking, and that man becomes aware that human mental capacities and corporeal forces now wield authority. Continuous, pulsating life, constant change, uninterrupted progress — these are important elements among the ideals and values of that which we call modernism. And consistent with historical fact, we can say that the last decades of the eighteenth century bring us to the threshold of a fundamental change in outlook. Secularization has come of age in the consciousness of Western man; the image of the City of God has faded, the foundations of the City of Man can now be laid.

Life in the modern world is like a journey on a river, always providing new landscapes, always beckoning to new adventures. There is an important psychological factor to be noted in this new state of consciousness; for in our biological and mental life there is always a menace hanging over us, that of sadness. Confronting this, modernism offers us a gift; this menace of depression and melancholy can be dispelled by activity, by change, by taking pleasure in change. In this way, modern man gives us a new concept, a new term: "radical" — because all of his strivings are directed to the *left*. The maxim of the French Revolution is *pas d'ennemi à gauche* — no enemies on the left.

Men of tradition are now in a serious situation. They face the threat of exclusion if they cling to their fathers' creed; and no one has articulated this better than de Tocqueville. Such people, he says, fear being abandoned and left alone with their ancient beliefs; and in this dilemma, fearing isolation more than error, they join the crowd (*Les hommes qui conservaient l'ancien foi craignirent d'être les seuls à lui rester fidèles, et, redoutant plus l'isolement que l'erreur, ils se rejoignirent à la foule sans penser comme elle*).

Modern man arrives on the scene with an inflated consciousness of being sovereign over his own interests. At the same time, he is sensual even though he believes himself to be rational. Is this confusion sufficient to serve as a legitimate basis for his new sovereignty over the earth? This demand for legitimacy is important; an answer to the question grows more urgent. In whose name and over whom will modern man hold dominion, legislate, and exercise power? Can this modern man be trusted? Traditional man had the roots of his personal identity in the divine order, guaranteed by the Almighty Father. But where can modern man find a new identity?

To say "identity" is to say "origin," for the word *identity* contains an implicit question: From whence do I come? Traditional man can answer without hesitation, for in the certainty of his belief he knows that he has his origin in the heavenly Father's creative act. Secularized man does not enjoy this certainty, even if he does not always deny its content. But paradoxically, this belief contains something that unites traditional and modern man; they both have the latent memory of a supernatural origin, of roots in beatitude, of a paradisal state that has been lost. Expulsion from Paradise means entry into the profane world, with all of its forms of limitation, contradiction, and conflict. But this primordial state of peace, serenity, and freedom from conflict lives on in man as a "memory." Thus man dreams of a lost Paradise, even in socialistic and communistic speculations — Karl Marx being no exception.

Man is a daydreamer. In many ways he moves in a landscape of fairy tales and dreams, an imaginary life that runs side by side with the hard brutality of life on this earth. He turns away from this ordinary world of conflict and struggle, this implacable labyrinth in which we wander; and he yearns for a peaceful and paradisal existence. Fairy tales and dreams can give what harsh, profane reality cannot provide. Unsubstantial hopes and fairy tales are a means to realize cherished dreams.

Are these cherished dreams only an escape from reality? The question cannot be answered unambiguously. Traditional man is conscious of the conditions that inexorably govern creation; he knows that the world is filled with contradictions and conflict; he knows that this brutal reality is a consequence of his expulsion from Paradise and that this is his destiny. He knows that a dream is a dream, that tales are tales, that the world is what it is, and that man is what he is — potentially a saint, potentially a villain. Traditional man knows that he cannot dream himself away from his earthly existence.

Secularized man, on the contrary, has lost this elementary wisdom. When he enters a world of tales and make-believe, the cherished daydream has a different content: Under the sign of the City of Man, almighty human power will realize terrestrial perfection. For secularized man not only lacks objective consciousness of the world as it actually exists — creation with all its limitations; more important, he also lacks a consciousness of the divine presence in the world and in the lives of men. He therefore senses an emptiness, a meaninglessness; and this stimulates him to give himself up to endless narcissistic imaginings and speculations. It is in these imaginings that daydream can replace reality. Traditional man, on the contrary, knows that the created world cannot become a paradise. But secularized man is enchanted by the dream that human power can eradicate existential imperfections.

One form of profane speculation is utopianism. Just as the scientist in his thinking and researches elaborates models as a means of subduing refractory nature, so the utopian builds ideal models for man and society, planning a complete profane order. During the baroque period in particular, utopian speculations had their heyday. We must note, however, that every utopia is a static model and not a living and practically useful social organism. And further, utopian systems were not meant to be put into actual use; rather, they were to be regarded as the "sovereign's mirror" whereby the potentates saw the defects of their own regimes by way of contrast.

Dreams and tales come and go, and utopian speculations make little if any contribution to the real world. The City of Man, steadily taking shape as a Gestalt in the eighteenth century, needed much more than dreams and fairy tales could possibly provide. The City of Man demands a constitution in a social, moral, and political sense. The elaboration of man's terrestrial power requires a higher, imperative authority; it needs a constitution that renders man's self-promotion legitimate, that gives him a "place" in his own consciousness, that reassures him concerning his own identity and legitimacy. But secularized man is one-dimensional man because he denies any higher, divine power; and thus it is within this one-dimensionality, this horizontality, that one must elaborate on the new constitution.

Essentially, the new constitutional order must resolve two problems. One concerns the emptiness we encounter in profane existence when the divine presence is forgotten, denied, or contested. And this vacuum, this absence of verticality, must somehow be eliminated on the horizontal, one-dimensional plane. The second problem is the vexing one of human identity; in his complex reality, man is simultaneously individual and transcendent; and this raises the question of how he can be at the same time both individual and universal.

The constitution that is to be elaborated must rise above all earthly homologies, all worldly connections, whether of time or space. This constitutional system must be above criticism, must transcend all doubt, and must not be bound to historical processes of change. It must have a transcendent authority that, in reality, only the Absolute can impart; an authority that will make this constitutional order immutable and universally valid. This means it must be a system with an authoritative power, which is possessed only by the sacred. This can be realized only in myth.

III

The Greeks have given us their name for the ancient concept that we know as myth. The Greek μῦθος, *mythos,* means the Word, the concrete authoritative tradition of a message concerning Reality, a message having the gods themselves as source. *Mythos* is predicative; sprung from a divine source, it provides humanity with what is valid and normative for activity in this world, for ways of thinking, for the making of laws. For the Greeks, myth expresses the totality of Being; and when Greek philosophy begins to take shape between the late seventh and the early sixth centuries B.C., myths still have this ancient meaning. In earlier ages, the Greeks included their Olympian gods and themselves in ontology; but the advent of philosophy and the philosophical manner of thinking means that they were beginning to depart from the ancient Oriental all-inclusive totality, from absolute, eternal Being and the implied Beyond Being. The journeying of Helios is a nonhistorical symbol for the steady, unchanging order of things. But henceforth the limited, the moderate, the temperate is to be the ideal; the boundless and unlimited is considered barbarous. The Judeo-Christian narration of Creation and of a loving and saving God will be regarded as something absurd, "unto the Greeks foolishness."

The Greek creates a myth about himself and his existence. The Aristotelian τὸ ὄν, *to on,* Being itself, is regarded as the ultimate, stable foundation and source; and this concept takes the place of the more universal Oriental totality from which it issues forth. Without using the name, even without consciousness of the content of the myth, it is nevertheless this philosophical commencement that secularized Western man begins to seek. And later, when the modernism of the eighteenth century insists on a constitution, we encounter a flood of literature asking for an unshakable rock on which to build the City of Man.

From all cardinal points and at all levels, philosophers and other authors try to find something capable of filling the vacuum left by the denial and loss of the divine order, the perception of the *kosmos*. With new geographical discoveries, Western man finds so-called natural, primitive peoples who are erroneously deemed to live without institutions, authority, or oppressors. Why not, like *le bon sauvage,* the good savage, live in the innocent bosom of nature? Another seductive notion is that truth is to be found like a "vein of gold"; and the hope of finding this "vein" of truth gave impetus to feverish philosophical search. Economic life was another field of promise: increasingly, men began to hope for "self-realization" from the dynamism of economic forces. But at the same time, ironically, among the so-called economists and physiocrats, we find the notion of an enlightened monarchical despot who rules the free economic forces with an iron hand.

None of these dreamers, tellers of tales, and utopianists ever came close to the great creative task that loomed before philosophy: namely, to build a new City, to give this City an adequate constitution, to bring man up and out of all terrestrial dependency and bondage, and to give him a new, immutable, and universally valid identity. The one who comes nearest to success in this enterprise of providing mankind its new "Magna Carta" is Jean-Jacques Rousseau.

A myth cannot have overmastering power unless it is "divinized"; it must "be," prior to all terrestrial existence. Such a myth must have its place in the primordial beginning of all things, in Being itself, the source of all that exists. Only this sacral, axiological originality renders the myth unalterable and universally valid. Rousseau achieved this; he invented a "paradisal" state of origin from which this myth issues forth, and he calls this state of origin Nature. Nature for Rousseau is the "sacral" point of departure for everything; in this state of Nature man is born free.

But this state of primordiality, this pure "sacral" Nature, is violated by human egotism and lust for power. This implies a brutal condition of struggle in which some have won power, while others have been enslaved. Those who hold this rough physical power translate it into justice and normative propriety. The subdued must obey. The Edenic landscape once given to the first men has been annihilated by the entry of brutal lust for power. Rousseau thus interprets the Fall as only a terrestrial drama, a secular tragedy. Man is born free and everywhere he is in chains. *L'homme est né libre, et partout il est dans les fers.*

What Rousseau understands as the innocent Paradise of Nature in reality involves the Judeo-Christian Fall, because the "liberty" that the first humans believe they must win by disobeying the command not to eat from the tree of the knowledge of good and evil is, in Rousseau's "paradise," the very foundation stone of human existence. And man's revolt against the dispositions of heaven, the attempt to "be like God," the equal of God, is the second foundation stone in Rousseau's "paradise." In his "sacral" order of Nature, Rousseau erects his dream-castle on two pseudo-archetypes: liberty and equality; and with these he builds the primordial foundation for what he preaches as terrestrial justice.

Man now has his objective: to overthrow what Rousseau regards as the "artificial" and "unjust" arrangement of things in which brutality and oppression dominate, and to bring creatures back to their "paradisal" origins, the order of Nature herself. Overthrowing injustice has, as a corollary, the positive aim of building up a constitution, of giving the "holy" order of Nature terrestrial legitimacy on the basis of the two "archetypes," liberty and equality.

But this demands a structure of rectitude, of natural right and justice, which in its turn demands manifestation. This discovery is the *Contrat social,* the Social Contract. Rousseau embraces the ancient idea that there is an innate order of justice in creation, a natural virtue and goodness; and this idea is certainly not absent from Western theology. Even the Gentiles, says St. Paul, have the law; and this deeply rooted principle of justice pervades the Middle Ages. But with its secularization in the baroque period, we are confronted with the notion of a profane natural right. The English social philosopher Thomas Hobbes shows the way with his treatise on sovereignty; and his compatriot, John Locke, advanced the cause further by introducing the double contract: first, a common one, and then a contract of sovereignty elaborated on the basis of the first.

These theoretical contracts, combined with utopian ideas and constructions, are efforts to introduce into ordinary, palpable life, into the practical world, institutions by which man can dominate and eliminate lawlessness and arbitrary oppression. First, Rousseau liberates the contract from its earthly, institutional, and political character; he elevates it to a mythic dignity, with the intention of abstracting it from its profane condition. For Rousseau, Nature is more than simply psycho-physical phenomena; she is *holy.* Liberty and equality likewise are holy and inalienable — Rousseau speaks of *la sainteté du contrat.*

All human beings are born equal, and thus one must rule out a social contract that includes sovereignty. The logical consequence is that everyone makes a contract with everyone else. By this contract everyone unites with everyone else, each gives himself up to the other, and in turn no one submits himself to anything or to any particular individual. Thus, power, oppression, and slavery are excluded. And thus if anyone should possess a right not also given to others, a tyranny would result and the social contract would be broken.

Rousseau apparently means that there is a kind of "secrecy" in this contract; everyone gains only the right that he has yielded to everyone else, and what is given is returned in reciprocity; or, as Rousseau puts it, mutuality. This mutuality engenders a state of both liberty and equality. Man is free in the sense that he is his own ruler, making his own laws; at the same time, in his "mutualism," he lives in equality — an equality that has a judicial prolongation: namely, citizenship. We cannot deny differences in power and intelligence; but this is Nature's own "injustice," which, Rousseau declares, finds compensation in the fact that everyone feels himself equal under the contract and in his citizenship — *ils deviennent égaux par convention et de droit.*

The development of this social contract requires Rousseau to proceed further down the road of pseudo-myth. Everyone will now have an associate status in the moral corporation, and not merely in a collectivity. The liberty of the individual is unchanged, but the contractual act excludes every form of social atomism and chaos because the social contract, as a moral corporation, is a unity; the contract-making multitude ascends to a higher "ego." By this "ascent," Rousseau adds another important element to the structure of his myth: Man's new power on this earth demands that his individuality, his "ego," be united with the collectivity that legitimizes his boundless earthly power. The individual and the collectivity must constitute a common identity. Man and Mankind will be one.

Rousseau has now resolved two fundamental constitutional problems. With the social contract he fills the vacuum we encounter when the traditional order is denied and abandoned; and he bridges the insupportable schism between the individual and the universal. The social contract is therefore much more than a judicial and moral act. The contract brings man — and therefore mankind — out of social bondage; man is elevated above all norms, above time and space, above all historical change and processes. The social contract thus has the elemental hallmarks of myth because it is, in its primordial origin, absolute. Man is "divinized": he has usurped the place of God.

The corporation, this higher "ego" that we now confront, manifests itself in the most varied forms, corresponding to the needs of the community. When this ego has to be an official personage, it is called the Republic or the political corporation. When passive, it is called the State or the City; and when in an active relationship, it is called Sovereign. Its collective and associative form is called the People, while in its individuality it is called the Citizen. And when considered under the law, it is called the Subject.

Rousseau uses the word *nature* in two senses: the original, just order of Nature; and the situation in which life is dominated by struggle, greed, oppression, and slavery. He makes a very important distinction here: Private life is not to be eliminated; indeed, it cannot be, for it pertains to human nature in its individual manifestation. But it is society, the human collectivity, where private interests and the desire for power dominate, which must be overcome by the social contract; and thereby man will be restored to his primordial purity and innocence. It is thus that Rousseau speaks of the sanctity of the social contract. But how is all this to be realized? Precisely here Rousseau faces a fundamental problem: dominion.

In Rousseau's scheme of things, dominion and oppression are inseparable. Dominion always means hierarchy, verticality. And here we are led to one of the summits of Rousseau's pseudo-mythical landscape. Dominion itself is to be abolished. The social contract accomplishes this stroke of magic; the contract is by nature egalitarian, and in virtue of this necessity no one can be oppressed.

Equality is the great peacemaker. But what is to be done with the manifestations of the corporation that, in collective form, we call the People, which in individual form we call the Citizen, and which is now presented as the State, now as Sovereign or Sovereignty? These ideas and institutions must be explained, they cannot be left to appear simply as political sphinxes. The State, the Sovereign, the People, the Citizen must be manifested and realized as a living corporation. And Rousseau bestows on it a life; he gives it a will, a higher Will — *la Volonté Générale*.

The social contract now becomes a living organism, having its own will; and this will is sacrosanct, expressing what the Sovereign People really intend. At the same time, it thereby expresses the common good. In a perversion of *vox populi, vox Dei,* the People's Will is exchanged for the Divine Will. The Sovereign People is not an enigmatic political sphinx. It is a living, higher ego; and its will realizes the terrestrial order, replacing the egotistic system of oppression with the primordially righteous State, thus expressing the inner meaning of *nature*.

This higher will must be realized in practice, however; it must enter the world in manifested forms. The sovereign citizens have to meet and determine, from a multitude of private meanings, what must develop into the *Volonté Générale*. Rousseau never denies that private interests exist; on the contrary, he says expressly that if private interests were not real the social contract would be superfluous. No, here we have a metamorphosis wherein human choices are elevated from the merely private to the general level, where the Popular Will is to be realized. But how?

Rousseau does not have a *Sanctum Officium,* a Papal Holy Office, nor a Stalinistic Politbureau at his disposal. Nor has he any authority founded on canonical Scriptures. But he tries to find and explain different ways in which this ascension can be accomplished. By deliberation, he says, it may be possible to bring a multitude of different opinions into concert. The more thoroughly we discuss a question, the more our differences can be reduced. By this means we can come nearer to what we want to achieve, namely unanimity; and unanimity expresses the Popular Will.

As men's interests are purely private, according to Rousseau, can there be any guarantee that merely exchanging ideas and opinions will accomplish a liberation of the ego from those interests? Seeking a way out of this dilemma, Rousseau tries to find support in his idea of mutuality, which already exists in the primordial social contract. When popular decisions are forthcoming, private interests will be treated as "pluses and minuses." What happens then? These pluses and minuses cancel one another, *ils s'entredétruisent*. The result of this politico-mathematical process will be the *Volonté Générale,* the General Will.

Rousseau is a master at manipulation, and he evidently means that we must find two ways out of all dilemmas and contradictions. His problem is to explain this miracle that lifts man out of his egoism and realizes his higher status as Citizen. One of these paths is the politico-arithmetic "plus and minus" preceded by penetrating discussions. The second is moral and psychological: the social contract has two cornerstones, the two "archetypes" of liberty and equality; and these exclude every form of oppression. A kind of harmony between the private and the general, between the individual and the official, thus arises from the social contract; and he declares a wonderful coincidence of interests and justice — *un accord admirable de l'intérêt et de la justice.*

In all of his prodigious myth building, it seems that when he must explain this metamorphosis from the private to the general, Rousseau waves the banner of Popular Will, definitively abolishing all antinomies that human individual and social life contain. But in all of his manipulations, he cannot avoid confronting the vote. Men must vote. And thereby we have majorities and minorities. What now becomes of this whole system of myth? It seems as though Rousseau loses his footing here. Instantly, what is called the highest Justice is seen to be naked Power. Power has returned. He who is of the minority is told by the majority that he has not rightly understood the real content of the Popular Will. *Cela ne prouve autre chose que je m'étais trompé.* The Stalinist Politbureau is prefigured. In Rousseau's one-dimensional world of popular Sovereignty there exists only a single will, a single truth, a single justice. And woe betide when you do not yield to it.

IV

The proclamation that there is a new sovereign on earth, Man, free and equal, Man who maintains the *Volonté Générale,* receives its perfect expression in Jean-Jacques Rousseau's doctrine of Social Contract. No more do we have to make do with tales, dreams, utopias; no, this perfected expression means that the proclamation of almighty Man is a myth rooted in the origin of existence itself, in Nature. The power proclaimed by the myth rests therefore on the foundation of liberty and equality, the two "archetypes" of Nature herself.

It is in the great French Revolution of 1789, the historical climax of a long process of secularization, that the proclamation of sovereign Man is made. Now myth must face up to reality; but revolutionary reality is not the Jacobin Club alone. No, it is in a polyvalent world that Rousseau's myth must be realized. The new dominant class, the third estate, is that of sensual man, man with all his selfish interests. And, not least, man with his economic interests is now making his entrance. Guided by objects of desire, this kind of man is more and more inclined to live in a multiversum; and growing economic liberty offers richer and richer possibilities for following the objects of desire, his personal lusts.

We must note that a great distance separates the new dominant class from that dreamer Rousseau, the man who proclaimed that money leads to slavery, the man who said *le mot de finance est un mot d'esclave.* The result is a foregone conclusion; the history of the Jacobin Club is short. The club's encounter with reality is not a romantic tableau of ancient Greek life where citizens of high political virtue and moral purity met in the *agora.* On the contrary, the third estate allows increasingly more scope for material interests. This new class, therefore, denies Rousseau's absurd and inherently contradictory system of spartan discipline, the perverse absorption of all private and all sensual activity by public life, following the expression of Malthus.

Does this mean that the glorious dream of sovereign, equal Man and his universal will is crushed? No, not at all. The world that is now developing, especially after the Napoleonic wars, involves profound mental and social changes. In short, one can characterize it as liberalism. Commercial development, improved communications, land reform, scientific and technological (i.e., industrial) progress — all of these factors lead men to believe in human progress. This new creed is given visionary form in the positivism of Auguste Comte. A new liberty has come into the world, and we must enjoy it to the full. There is no *Volonté Générale* to rein in the free play of human forces. As Max Weber says, we now lay the foundation of modern society; we distinguish the private from the public.

Can we now, perhaps, say that Rousseau's magnificent

edifice lies in ruins? Not at all. Liberty and equality, the two "archetypes," live on with undiminished power; and the Popular Will more and more expresses the real power in the affairs of this earth. It is a question of new forms being molded for the expression of these "archetypes." Rousseau provides building materials for the new world of ideas from which the nineteenth century is being formed: the ideologies.

It is very important here to distinguish between myth and ideology. Myth is an intelligible structure, an arrangement independent of the will and striving of the individual. Myth is based on a primordial, paradisal state; it is transcendent, standing before man as if it were elevated over every form of earthly appetitive life, above all imperfections and oppositions. Myth is absolute and does not admit of contradictions; it is total, universal, unlimited, high above time and space. It is nonhistorical in origin. Philosophically, myth reposes in pure existence. It is a commanding, ontological power before which man has no choice but to obey.

Ideology, on the contrary, is a frankly worldly system, and the material with which it is built belongs to the order of created things. Ideologies participate in the permutations of existence; they are integrally involved in time and space, taking part in the struggles and contradictions of the world. Indeed, ideology is itself a part of these contradictions, even if its goal is to bring all antinomies into a harmonious unity. The myth is "that which is"; but the significance of an ideology is determined by historical and existential becoming.

In this new world that is opening up under the impulsions and potentialities of liberty, liberalism becomes the natural ideological form of expression. Bourgeois liberalism is propelled by rational and sensual individualism, rationally scheming, free to "realize" itself hedonistically, and it is controlled by self-interest. In this coherence of the rational and the passionate

39

is formed the ideology that we call Western liberalism, which manifests itself as an attitude, as a philosophy, as a doctrine of social life, and as economic doctrine. Liberalism is first of all a manifestation of liberty. Now liberty is not only freedom of choice, it is also liberty in an absolute sense. This means that it has its roots in a higher order; it is a property of humanity itself, deciding man's manner of thinking and acting. Liberty possesses an intrinsic value. De Tocqueville has this in mind when he says: He who seeks something else in liberty than liberty itself is doomed to slavery — *qui cherche dans la liberté autre chose qu'elle même est fait pour servir.*

In Rousseau's myth system liberty is one and indivisible; simultaneously individual and universal, it is elevated high above all earthly limitations. The liberty that we encounter in what we call ideological liberalism, on the contrary, is earthly; it belongs to the sensory order, the created world; and therefore it can be given a social, national, collective, or individual content and meaning. But before all else, liberty is the property of every individual; and as such it is the fundamental element in the idea of human identity. In the ideological doctrine that we call liberalism, human identity is founded exclusively on the individual. Liberalism thus rests on an atomistic conception of the human being.

But the atomistic individual, entering the multiversum, does not bring the world to chaos. The liberal man, declaring himself a self-governing entity, is the dynamic wellspring of power in the modern world, continuously calculating and rationally adapting and exploiting a ceaselessly growing mass of experience. In a world of sensualism, he is always choosing the pleasant, toward which man is inherently inclined; and he likes to believe that his choices are always directed toward what is best in the long term.

The liberal man is also a citizen, and in his social life and activity he cannot avoid this question: What is true and what is false? As John Stuart Mill says, truth is an endless number of fragments in which true and false are mingled. But the golden grains of truth can be sifted out; and this is accomplished by the unending, reiterated exchange of opinions. The lifeblood of liberalism, therefore, is debate and discussion. Every restraint, every limit on opinion must be denied; for only what every human individual perceives sensually and rationally, through the use of his sense faculties, only this constitutes his "self-realization" and only this is right and valid. If debate is checked or stopped, this "truth" withers away. Thus, for the Spanish diplomat Juan Donoso Cortes, the liberal bourgeois class is a "discussing class," *clase discutadora.* In this continual exchange of opinion among free individuals, liberalism says, citizenship is formed. And the loftiest form of this exchange is institutionalized in parliamentary bodies, the representative community.

The aim of citizenship is first of all to defend liberty and property, spiritual as well as material. For the concept of property — the word being conceived in its widest possible sense — belongs to the individual who in himself is his own identity. Property and the individual are one. Property therefore has not only a judicial but also a moral meaning. Life in the world of liberalism is a private concern before all else.

In the same way that we win the truth and thereby provide for ourselves a foundation of rational life, so must we shape economic life. The free exchange of goods, freedom of communication by road, by sea — all of this will involve the entire world in the exchange of goods. Just as there will be a perpetual exchange on the so-called intellectual level, what John Stuart Mill calls the constant clash of opinions, where (it is postulated) truth always wins out over error, so in the same way economic freedom will bring us the best and most useful goods.

Liberalism is founded on certain distinct postulates that, nevertheless, are seldom discussed and even less frequently are critically examined. Often, not even the so-called intellectuals are aware of them. I mention three of these fundamental assumptions: First, every human individual is regarded as an inexhaustible well of energy, an active being dominated by mundane interests and by ascendancy of the rational element in human nature, always directing his energy toward sane and lucid goals. But is there not a danger that subconscious and involuntary forces in humanity may gain an upper hand and that man will become passive and succumb to the domination of pleasure and mere ingestion, to consumerism? Alexis de Tocqueville and John Stuart Mill discussed this possibility in an interesting correspondence. A possible resolution of their debate might be that liberalism continually offers new objectives for different kinds of human activity and for diverse sensory enjoyment; in short, there is incessant change. Liberal man avoids mere passivity because life in the liberal scheme of things constantly offers new avenues of activity and new opportunities for sensory experience.

The second "hidden" postulate is that the free play of diverse forces always produces a state of harmony and equilibrium. The generous production of goods and their free exchange result in stable prices that, in turn, issue into the market equilibrium of supply and demand. In these conditions, the pursuit of private gain by innumerable individuals does not result in chaos, but rather in social mobility and a desirable circulation of classes and goods, and to social harmony as well. For the needs of each individual are supplied by another individual's pressing desire for gain — or so the theory has it. This is similar for the innumerable transactions that make up liberal social life. Liberal man, with his rational calculations, his empirical trial and error, with greed as his lodestar, thus produces — despite himself, one might say — a harmony between merely private and public interests, between personal and collective life. In the end, liberalism means cosmopolitanism, free exchange between peoples and nations; not only of material goods, but also of spiritual values (it is alleged). Therefore liberalism presents itself as a doctrine of peace among men.

The third postulate is the doctrine of the positivity of truth. The liberal mind does not believe in a knowledge that is superior or anterior to reason; intelligence, too, is atomistic. We must therefore arrive at our understanding of truth and justice by means of our own intellectual, that is, rational, efforts. Man tries to find truth because he accepts the notion that if one knows the truth, one acts on it, a Socratic notion that modern liberalism has misunderstood. Continual searching and re-searching, gathering raw data, empirical trials, analysis through logical and discursive processes of thinking, always in a cadre of continuous debate: These are the operative demands of the liberal search for truth — truth which, it is believed, is like grains of gold, washed and sifted in a free selective process, the false dross being separated from the noble metal of truth.

Liberalism is thus the purest form of positivism. It will sustain a world of freedom in which truth will win out over the lie. The human spirit, says liberalism, finds itself only when in full freedom it searches for truth and justice. In the same way, the best goods are produced and brought to market. This positivist view is linked, partially at least, with two notable ideas: that of unending development, that is to say, uninterrupted progress; and the notion that what is regarded as truth participates in this progress: the true will become better and better, ever more "true."

Liberalism encounters the new Europe, a Europe that is more and more open to the free play of economic forces. But in the nineteenth century, liberalism is set amid a residual order of political, social, cultural, and spiritual hierarchies. Over against liberal republicanism stand the feudal and monarchical remains from the traditional order, forces that seek restoration. Liberalism must try to win over these forces. But this is not all; the new productive processes of Western industrialization entail urbanization. This marks the origin of a new social class, the proletariat; and this situation, in turn, brings liberalism into a new conflict situation.

V

First, industrialism means the division of the production process into segments; second, it means the mechanization of these processes. In traditional, preindustrial production, tools are made to complement the human hand and arm. Extensions of human faculties, they are made in the measure of man who is in no way diminished by their use. In production by the artisan, the processes are synthetic. The artisan begins with his concept of the whole, and on this basis "synthesizes" the materials and components that enter into the whole, making them into a final product, a unity. The sources of energy are mostly human or are at least subordinated to human faculties. The operation, however, is not "humanistic"; though the intelligence of the artisan dominates the operations involved — selecting and preparing materials, directing the tools — he is himself guided by intelligence of a higher order. *Ars sine scientia nihil.* And we must note in particular that the artisan determines the rhythm and pace of the productive processes, which, like the tools, are made to the measure of man.

The mechanization of industrial processes means that the source of energy — and, *a fortiori*, the presiding idea — are outside of and apart from the artisan. It means that machines and no longer man determine both the order of production and its final result. The human contribution will be atomized into numerous incomplete operations, most of them deprived of any qualitative element. Man may not become entirely passive in productive work, but he is nevertheless degraded; in a mechanized world, man becomes the servant of the machine.

Traditional labor is a qualitative labor; it creates a product that integrally bears the imaginative, creative stamp of the craftsman. Traditional labor thus has an aesthetic content as well, for no one in his right mind strives to bring forth ugliness. At the same time, it has a moral or ethical content in the sense that an ever-present aim is to produce something worthy; for bad workmanship and carelessness always evoke contempt and condemnation. Traditional labor can be and is linked to the transcendent; human labor can be a celebration of the Creator, for it can be regarded as a mimesis — doubtless with all its earthly deficiency — of the work of the Creator. In traditional labor we encounter true joy in work, and most often, and not by accident, we hear the rhythmic songs occasioned by this joy.

Mechanized labor annihilates these values. We find in their stead all of the dominating considerations of economic value, implying a manner of life that is profanely conceived, a life lived "by bread alone," a life that receives its benediction in political economy. Mechanized labor has as its most elementary sign the rotating wheel. Now the center of the wheel is the hub, which allows the wheel to rotate, and in this rotation the periphery is the essential for modern industrial processes. The more rapid the peripheral movement, the greater the material production and vice versa.

The mechanization of labor is not only a degradation of man; much worse than that, it is a tragedy. But the inhabitants of the City of Man must conceal and atone for this tragedy. They will do this in two ways. The first is an effort to avoid pain, rough and heavy physical work. Machines will replace old-fashioned drudgery, and their greater productive capacity will multiply profit and contribute to higher living standards. Second, they will increase so-called leisure time, bringing man pleasure and happiness, not to speak of the humanist illusion that an increase of leisure brings with it cultural amelioration. More and more energy will be freed from fatiguing labor. When the plow advances by itself through the field, and the shuttle through the warp — then man will be truly free, according to Aristotle.

The mechanization of human work, with the purely economic ends that are implied, entails a fundamental alteration in social interchange: namely, the loss of patriarchalism. Traditional working life involved patrons and masters who had the obligations of the patriarchal function, including that of custody for their workers — however insufficiently and uncharitably these may have been carried out. The capitalist (whether state, private, or mixed) industrial system annihilates all of this; patriarchal bonds are broken. In a world dominated by machines, by the owners of capital, and by the struggle for profit, the morale of the proletariat is marked by a sense of abandonment. Not only has the worker been disenfranchised as a producer through the mechanization of productive life, he has also been "atomized" socially. He is the bastardized slave of the machine; and here we see the "fate" of the modern industrial proletariat that Karl Marx describes with the Hegelian terms *Entfremdung* and *Entäusserung*: respectively, alienation or estrangement, and renunciation, relinquishment, or termination of property rights.

In the bosom of bourgeois liberal society, a new social class comes into existence, and in this very fact the third estate's liberalism faces a new negation. Liberalism, individualism, and atomism are no solution for this new class, and therefore the people demand a new system of belief: Socialism is born in a new surge of ideology.

Socialism in general and Marxism in particular draw radical conclusions from the two great changes — the loss of fatherhood and the mechanization of labor — that industrialism brings in its wake. The worker has been deprived of his tools and is estranged from the new, giant apparatuses of production; and it is at this point that Marx introduces his Hegelian *Entfremdung,* estrangement of alienation. Further, the capitalist, the owner of the productive apparatus, imperatively needs the worker; he, the worker, must in turn "sell" not only his productive power but also his human dignity as producer. Here Marx introduces the Hegelian *Entäusserung,* the relinquishment or alienation of property.

As for the problems of ownership, a return to a preindustrial status is impossible because the capitalist-industrial system requires both private ownership and a collective form of production. Thus a reconciliation between labor and capital must itself be collective. Therefore, say the socialists, the answer lies in a productive community, a fellowship of the productive apparatus. Marx declares that by this socialization, man will become free, delivered from the damnation of *Entfremdung* and *Entäusserung.* According to Marx, man is not only tied to productive forces, he is by origin a universal being, united with this world, with mankind; he is, as Marx says, following his mentor Hegel, a *Gattungswesen,* a collective being, a collective personality, living in a kind of mystical unity with the world itself. In this way, then, man is tied to his own life as worker and, consequently, is united with his tools. To the question, What is man?, Marx answers: Man is a producer. Is this the way that Marx proposes to solve the problem of man's atomization and alienation in industrial society? In a fantasy of simplistic Hegelian dialectic, capitalism explodes. Socialism will show us the road to the original, primordial, and just order of production: the elimination of the capitalist system, the last antagonistic form of the productive process in society. Marxism holds that by this institutional revolution the unfailing road to human liberation and human happiness will open before us.

The second great challenge, the loss of patriarchalism, means for Marx a liberation from every kind of hierarchy. All that is vertical and transcendent in human existence will be replaced by the horizontality of brotherhood. We must freely associate labor, with its community of property, with distribution according to the principle that everyone must produce what he is able to make and that everyone will receive according to his needs. All of this is to be accomplished in an order of brotherly solidarity in which, simultaneously, the individual achieves — in Hegelian terms — "self-realization." Just as with liberalism, socialism proclaims that reality is one-dimensional. There is no power commanding human life higher than man himself. Liberty, equality, and fraternity are the lodestars for both of these nineteenth-century ideologies. Both have inherited from Rousseau the notion of human sovereignty; and for both, liberty and equality are original, prerational, primordial pseudo-archetypes. The free and the equal are regarded as fundamental ingredients in the historical process.

But there are essential differences between liberalism and socialism. For the liberal, freedom and equality are potentialities, starting points for individual as well as social life. For the socialist, freedom and equality are final goals because only when socialist transformation is realized, when "alienation" is eliminated, can man be free. The liberal thinks in terms of the individual, atomistically; the socialist thinks in terms of the collectivity. The liberal thinks positively; the socialist thinks dialectically.

These differences are important when we consider the notion of citizenship. The liberal citizen is an individual, the dynamic well of energy in the social order; and the corresponding civic aims are to defend life and liberty and the property of the individual. The communal civic effort, therefore, will be the sustained endeavor to defend and conserve these values, first of all by parliamentary debates. Liberal citizenship is political.

For the socialist, citizenship is won first of all by eliminating the conflicts and antagonisms of society, by placing production — the word is used here in its widest possible sense — in the hands of the whole people. The liberal lives individualistically in the world that surrounds him. Socialist citizenship is integral, when it is achieved. Man and labor, man and nature, man and society, all enter into a dialectical unity, into a cosmic solidarity. It is in this cosmic solidarity that man, in the socialist meaning, enters society as a citizen, a trustee, integrally and actively taking part in all fields of existence. The Marxist regards politics, conceived in its liberal meaning, with its public institutions and its debating parliaments, as a centralized system of coercion that will disappear when integral, governing citizenship is realized. Then, as Friederich Engels says, *der Staat stirbt ab,* the State will pass away.

These two dominant nineteenth-century ideologies, liberalism and socialism, are impressive in their vitality. Though both are varied and manifold, both also constitute a negation of all that remains of the old traditional order; they are *ecclesiae militantes,* church militants, and therefore are often found in intimate collaboration against tradition, their common enemy. But at the same time they are deeply and reciprocally in conflict. Both are founded on sturdy cornerstones. One of these is man, a strong indivisible unity, a center of energy and consciousness, dominated by his individual interests, and with his indomitable will striving for "self-realization" — in liberalism an individual goal, but in socialism a collective one. The second cornerstone, society, is in fact an extension of the first. In liberalism, society is the locus of all human activity and is where every form of progress is realized. In socialism, sensate man's aim is to find his dialectic unification with and in a noncontradictory cosmos.

Secularization progresses through the nineteenth century, amid all of the smoke from ideological flames; and this growing worldliness is reflected in the ever-recurring compromises of theology, in its strategic and tactical retreats. Man is regarded as essentially a corporeal and mental entity, monadic and invariable; it is presumed that he always has a stable ground underfoot in permanent social circumstances. All of these assumptions, this hubris, contribute to belief in a general, undeviating progress; no failures, no deceptions, no doubts can win man away from this cherished belief. "Go forward, humanity. Be happy, be solaced. For you carry eternity in your bosom," sings the Swedish poet, Viktor Rydberg.

VI

Symbolically speaking, traditional man lives "between Heaven and Earth." Certainly he is conditioned by his terrestrial bonds; but simultaneously, he lives under a higher, divine dispensation. He can conform to and obey these providential arrangements because he himself participates in a luminous and secret immortality that conveys to him his consciousness and knowledge that his sensory and mental faculties cannot provide in and of themselves. Man consists of body, soul, and spirit: the Greek *soma, psyche, nous;* the Latin *corpus, anima, spiritus.* The

Spirit, *nous,* Meister Eckehart's *intellectus,* gives man his central value and dignity, raising him above the limitations of the merely sensory and psychic orders and giving to his intelligence the capacity of objectivity and the possibility of contemplating the Divine. Thanks to these qualities, man can distinguish between the real and the unreal, between truth and untruth, between good and evil.

When man affirmatively and effectively recognizes his higher destiny, he gains a new, sober, and nobler personal unity, a higher ego, a reflection of the Self of esoterism. His sensual ego, his corporeal and mental capacities, are certainly not denied by this, for they are homologous elements in the integral human individual; but they are subordinated to the spiritual Self. Reason, will, the life of the senses and of the imagination — all of these concur in and provide terrestrial confirmation of the consciousness-giving spiritual Light. This means that man has a higher knowledge, a spiritual insight that is intuitive in the sense of being suprarational and not determined by logical, discursive, experiential criteria. Yet this higher knowledge is at the same time linked with our sensory, earthly capacities, all of which have an active role to fulfill in man's spiritual life. It is thus that we can say that man lives "between Heaven and Earth."

Secularization initially enters the life of mankind not so much by direct denial of the Divine, but rather by making man himself co-equal with God. In paradise, the serpent does not ask man to deny God, he says only that man can be "like God." In this effort to be the analogue of the Divine, it is necessary to mobilize the earthly, sensate forces in man's nature, and first of all sensuality and reason, *sensus* and *ratio.*

The triumphal march of secularization has many phases. The scientific and technological successes of the baroque era were supposed to redound only to the Heavenly Power, *ad majorem Dei gloriam.* No philosophers or scientists aim to dethrone the King of heaven. Not even the most far-reaching political revolutions — before 1917 — dare to exclude the celebration of the Almighty; and the various ideologies gain much power by taking unto themselves "paradisal" notions and dreams. But the road to secularization leads implacably to a premeditated devolution of energies, which are then deployed on the sensate level. One of the fundamental postulates in this triumphal "progress" is that, corporeally and mentally, man is a fixed and indivisible unity. Is man, in fact, anything besides a sum of physical and psychic forces? This reductive question is already posed in the French Revolution of 1789, and is an ill-omened query.

Again, man is conceived as dynamic but fixed, a centrum of energies; to this is added a conception of society that is assumed to be similarly unchanging. Traditional society was a human community on all levels; but even in all of its mundane complexity, traditional society was not a chaos because it was ruled by a higher, divine order. Traditional society was molded in cultic forms, a cult that expressed the truth that man had to accept and to obey the heavenly norms or suffer the consequences. The social hierarchy also reflected this order; it was equipped with the power of command and enforcement and required obedience. Earthly and social power was a reflection of the divine order. Traditional society was therefore an interplay between vertical and horizontal forces.

This idea was not altogether absent even as late as the twentieth century, even if it was more and more called into question. A living society must, on the one hand, have a harmonious interplay between freedom and equality; and on the other, it must have the hierarchical principles of value and order. There must be a harmony between a self-interested and an unselfish citizenry, between independence and obedience.

52

Three fundamentals are to be found in a traditional society: first, a spiritual, cultic community combined with a consonant moral consciousness; second, social solidarity extending beyond all particular interest groups and organizations; and third, an ethnic and historical affiliation, wherein memories serve to unite men in a sense of common inheritance and readiness to sacrifice.

Secularism postulates that man is a fixed, indivisible, and dynamic center of forces; to this is added the belief that society represents an inalienable and stationary order. The optimism and belief in progress of the nineteenth century found support in these postulates. Millions were attracted to contemporary ideologies. Romanticism, humanism, and countless idealistic movements (so called) all gave generations hope for betterment, peace, and freedom. We must be aware of how these movements, in their marvelous vitality, profoundly influenced and changed the whole nineteenth century. Powerful and, as it seemed at the time, victorious ideologies lit incense, so to speak, and wrapped themselves in fragrant smoke, concealing motives of egoism and pleasure-seeking that they really sought to advance. These climates of opinion impressed on society their daydreams, proclaiming themselves the bearers of a citizenship that in reality they undermined by secret egoism and competing selfish interests, all the while weakening the forces of unselfishness, which are the only real basis for citizenship.

Now, as we reach the close of the twentieth century, it becomes increasingly more apparent that these ideologies, bearers of generations of enthusiasm and vitality, are losing their strength. The two received fundamentals and the two seemingly inexhaustible sources of power, namely the human individual and an unshakable social order, begin to waver in the mind-sets and aims that sustained them. More and more, the magnificent romantic view of man is replaced by the ambitions of individuals and of groups, focused on very narrow interests. Society, this *societas humana,* is menaced by accelerating economic and technological developments and, in the political and social order, by proliferating bureaucracy. Within this world of bureaucracy a modern Leviathan is rising: the all-competent State.

Society is a living organism and properly should be the carrier of a hierarchy of values, of unshakable spiritual and moral norms; society is of the qualitative order. But this commonwealth is now threatened with replacement by a centralized world of bureaucracy whose aim is to dominate the vacuum that a withering civilization is leaving behind. The modern industrial and social state is quantitative in nature and, as centralized bureaucracy, it has no moral norms. The aim of the modern state is to intervene continuously and to regulate the secular order wherein sensate interests are increasingly dominant. Once upon a time, in traditional societies, laws were complements and confirmations of an order of things that had its profoundest roots in the spiritual realm and in a social morality deriving from that realm. Now we see the opposite: A feverish, administering, regulating, legislating activity becomes unavoidable, and the power of the state necessarily grows apace. Economic and productive life also calls forth administrative and bureaucratic pyramids. The scope for responsible citizenship is steadily eroded; man will become more and more a subject.

It is an irony of destiny that new scientific theories relating to the world of particle physics have had a deep effect on twentieth-century thought at the same time that the venerable conception of the natural order, valid for centuries, is no longer fully in force. The new foundation stone of existence, the atom, is no longer what it once was. The new physical tableau of the world, linked with such names as Max Planck, Albert Einstein,

Werner Heisenberg, Erwin Schrödinger, and many others, offers a conception of physical reality that, according to Heisenberg, is more akin to that advanced by Heracleitus more than twenty-five hundred years ago: "You cannot step twice into the same waters, for other waters are ever flowing in." For modern physical theory, at least, this means that creation is reduced to a level even lower than its constituent sensory elements; nothing can be said to be anything else, ultimately, than an "atomistic" multiversum. Consequently, man is conceived as a being lacking any primary substance; he is nothing other than an "inner flux" whose mental and corporeal faculties are mere functional details.

In the middle of the twentieth century, this novel and doubtless volatile view receives a comprehensive, mathematical and technological interpretation: cybernetics. Its leading exponent, Norbert Wiener (1874–1964), offers us a view of existence as a riverine landscape. The principal reality is chance; but there are islands where, with our scientific and technical activity, we can take up residence. Man's primary task, in this universal and accidental flux, is to find ways and means for information, communication, and control. He has machines at his disposal, he has organizing talents; and organization is necessary for man as well as for society. Life, therefore, is a struggle for order, and order is necessary for survival; and at present, survival means the maximum exploitation of technology. Humanistic ideas such as "life" and "soul" lose their meaning because both are reduced to the nervous system, which operates according to the same principles as do binary, electronic machines, both being merely apparatuses. The alternatives these machines "choose" are selected on the basis of prior performance. From the "viewpoint" of the binary, mathematical machine, the individuality of the soul consists in persisting memories and instructions, and these mental processes develop along previously evolved courses.

According to Wiener, to live means to be receptive to a continuous stream of influences from the environment, to the stimuli of the milieu. Thus we are only elements in a process. To "live" is to participate in all that is happening in the world, to take part in an uninterrupted development of knowledge — a "knowledge" that is never conclusive but is forever in process, forever becoming. We *are* elements of communication, media whose cogs and strata are human organisms; thus it is of very little significance whether the fundamental material is human or mechanical. Such is the conclusion of Norbert Wiener. Consequently, principial differences between man and machine do not exist. A machine can be connected with another machine without human intervention; and by electronic or mechanical circuitry, a machine can exercise "self-control." Wiener was a mathematician and physicist; thinking along these lines led him to believe that fluidity and chance are major factors determining human life on this earth. We have to find our abodes on "islands of entropy," as he says, where we can live with our information, our communications, and our controls over the chaotic flux of existence. In this "cybernetic" life, according to Wiener, we live and act in essentially the same manner as do machines.

Wiener can be regarded — and dismissed — as a cynic. But in reality, he only provides, possibly in an extreme form, a mathematico-physical interpretation of modern man and his entire existential situation in the presumed universal flux, a flux that lacks any foundation whatsoever. What must be understood is that modern man, in his secularization, lives in a one-dimensional universe wherein his mental and corporeal energies and faculties are, as outlined above, only functional details. In this existential situation, the integral human individual is reduced to the sum of his functions; in effect,

56

condemned to an existence in which chance is the dominant feature. And in this accidental world, what can be said to be good, what bad?

What Wiener describes in his "cyberneticism" is the Western predicament as revealed initially by modern science. Wiener describes this predicament mathematically, even while giving it a symbolic interpretation. This situation, however, demands a more ample explication, a total interpretation of existence that contemporary Western man will find valid. Such an interpretation not only must be founded on a scientific, quantitative point of view; it must also unify man and the world in which he lives.

This pretentious aim requires us to rise above all particular branches of science and their specialized perspectives, an occasion that provides an entry for profane speculative philosophy. In this new task philosophy must try to interpret man's world, and the interpretation must be both historical and pioneering. An adequate philosophical system must explain man and his condition; it must take into account and unify prior ideas, movements, and aspirations, showing where man comes from and where he is going. In other words, such a system must concurrently open doors to an enlarged consciousness of existence, a Gestalt of reality; and it must prepare a consciousness that at the same time is linked to historical roots and can serve as a guiding star.

The prevailing outlook of Western secularism is the result of a historical process, at least on the obvious level. It expresses the consciousness of modern man, in whose view existence is a reductionist "nothing more," a "heracleitic" unidimensional flux. For modern man, nothing is superior to current, received opinion. It is this one-dimensional flux that will be dressed up in philosophical costume. We are, as it were, "waiting for Godot," waiting for the Philosopher of the City of Man.

VII

The German philosopher Martin Heidegger (1889–1976) provides the most ample philosophical statement of the new outlook. He is for the twentieth century what Hegel was for the nineteenth and what Kant was for the eighteenth. In his most important work, *Sein und Zeit* (1927; published in 1962 in English translation as *Being and Time*), Heidegger represents reality as a one-dimensional existential flux. The starting point for his philosophy is the language (but not the reality) of ancient Greek ontology, the effort to explain Being as the most general of all concepts. Being is the foundation of existence, that from which existence springs forth; *existence* is Heidegger's central concern. Being, the Aristotelian τὸ ὄν, *to on*, cannot be defined; it is obscure, says Heidegger. When we ask what Being "is," we do not know what "is" means. There is nothing superior to Being — which is itself horizontal and one-dimensional and which therefore includes both heaven and hell, celestial and infernal states.

As Being includes all existence, our existence, our life can be nothing more than one modality, *Seinsmodi*, among other modalities of existence. And these *Seinsmodi*, in Heidegger's expression, must be strictly separated from Being itself. Being is the essence of life, of the existential — *Wesensverfassung des Daseins*, in Heidegger's words. But what he calls existence, *Dasein* (= "being there") — what is it? Well, life is existence; but this kind of existence, when it exists, is found in consciousness only. And here we have a formulation typical of Heidegger.

Does existence (*Dasein*, "being there") have a meaning? Yes: *Zeitlichkeit*, "the timely." We can understand what existence essentially means, as Being, only when we grasp this "timeliness," this *Zeitlichkeit*. Even if we are incapable of grasping Being itself as essence, we can nevertheless get an idea of Being, immersed as it is in existence, from the experience of time. The phenomenon we call "time" is at the root of all of the knowledge we possess of the problems of existence; it is in time that we can distinguish the various "sectors" of our existence. We live in the current of time, which means that our existence is "that which was." Existence, in other words, is the past. If we must speak of meaning in connection with Being, we find it in temporality, *Zeitlichkeit,* in the current of history. There are no firm points in our existence; all is in flux. We step into a river, but even as we do so, it is no longer the same river; for, as Heracleitus said, other waters are ever flowing on. Or in the words of Norbert Wiener, we are ourselves floating in an ocean of entropy.

Where does man enter this picture? And how? According to Heidegger, it is by speech. The Greek word *logos,* Word, implies not only verbal activity, speaking; it also has broader, more ambiguous, and more profound senses, as both Plato and Aristotle attest. St. John, too, clearly indicates this in the Prologue of his recension of the gospel. *Logos* means intellect, idea, reason, discourse, definition, judgment. But Heidegger annihilates all of these more profound meanings of the word; for him, the term is univocal, having only a single and simple meaning: the activity of talking. But this talking, Heidegger's *Rede,* is necessarily linked to what has been apprehended; talking concerns what has been beheld. To talk is to communicate experience by the use of words.

Talking means connection with another person, contact with someone else. But at the same time the important thing, says Heidegger, is that talking is linked with something seen or experienced, and this is what he calls a synthesis. But synthesis is not to be regarded as a psychical or mental process, an inner observation and assimilation of something external. No, it is only that the seen, the experienced, is linked to something else; that which is experienced is linked to that which is articulated. What is happening here? Not the true correspondence between object and mind, between experience and speech, between what is experienced and what is said. No, what occurs is that existence, *Dasein,* will be brought forth from the hidden and the unknown; in short, *Dasein,* "being there," will be discovered. This is of fundamental importance: By bringing something out into the daylight, so to speak, it is existentiated and thereby becomes true. The corollary is that what is not existentiated is false in that it is concealed. In this way Heidegger answers the question, What is Truth? Truth, for Heidegger, is sensation, perception.

The conclusion is that what we observe is what is true. Truth, in other words, is the world of phenomena, the ever-shifting world of things. Knowledge of existence, an ontology of sorts, is possible only when it is conceived as phenome-nology. Being is hidden behind the scenes, but phenomena are manifested and "seen"; they constitute the "existence of the Being," as Heidegger says. Being itself, that which is hidden, Heidegger calls transcendence; but we are not to understand this in the Scholastic sense nor as the Greeks conceived it. Rather, for Heidegger Being is "ecstatic" — by which he means that it is outside of the phenomenal order. We humans are therefore confined within a horizontality that perforce separates us from Being itself, living as we do in the world of phenomena.

Is this phenomenal world, this world of things, as con-ceived in our highest consciousness, the world of reality? No, says Heidegger, higher than this reality is the possible. If we are to understand phenomenology properly, we must regard it as possibility. What does this mean? When we speak of the world of phenomena, this "world" has a fundamental structure, "to-be-in-the-world," *in-der-Welt-sein,* which is aprioristic, not based on experience. The world is everlasting. And I live in this world; but this "I" cannot be regarded as an individually limited substance, which means that what we call "I" cannot be separated from others, from "one another." Indeed, as existence is but a great current of time, how could such separation be possible? In this existential flow, we encounter the possible; the human "I" takes part in this and is one with existence, *Dasein*, "being there," because existence is an unbroken stream. And this implies that what we call "I" has unlimited possibilities. Existence is mine, and at the same time it is the stream of possibilities. This position of man in existence makes it possible for him to choose.

In this existential flow there is only subjectivism. This is one of the fundamentals of Heidegger's philosophy. Objectivity cannot exist because it presupposes an existential equilibrium, and such an equilibrium in turn presupposes an interplay between verticality and horizontality, to speak macrocosmically. Or to express it microcosmically, it presumes an inner and an outer. But Heidegger's philosophy proclaims a one-dimensional existence and, consequently, total subjectivism in a continuous stream. This radical subjectivism annihilates all boundaries between the ego — the "I" — and existence at large, existence itself. When we ask "who" a man is, says Heidegger, we might as well ask "what" existence is. Between man and existence, there is total community.

In this subjective totality, the ego — the "I" — meets "others" — fellow beings; but in a world without lines of demarcation, I cannot differentiate or separate myself from those others, fellow beings, because all of us exist in common with our world. When I talk with myself, it is really existence that speaks to me. What I conceive as the ego in a spatial sense is only an existential space. In the same way, my fellow beings are not at all to be regarded as personalities, as our associates, but rather as mere modalities of existence. Even when I am alone, with no companion, "I" am always with the world, says Heidegger. I am in a state of contact, *Mitsein,* and when we speak of "others" we do not think of certain concrete persons: everyone is interchangeable with anyone whomsoever. "The other *[der Andere]* is a double of the self" — this statement is a typical formulation of Heidegger's. As human individuals, we are thoroughly replaceable; this is a consequence of his anthropology.

Heidegger further confirms this interchangeability in his terminology. If we ask who is "who"?, this does not refer to myself, to another person, or even to the sum of all persons; no, "who" is a neuter, "man," as in the German *das Mann.* But we are not to regard this human neuter as something general, something abstract or subjective; on the contrary, *Das Mann* is a neuter expressing the average, *Durchschnittlichkeit,* of human existence as a unidimensionality. In this neutrality it is totally impossible for a human individual to be distinguished or elevated in any sense, and here we have Heidegger's egalitarian gospel. Every priority is excluded: *jeder Vorrang wird geräuschlos niedergehalten.*

Heidegger deeply disdains psychology and psychic phenomena; nevertheless, he himself introduces a mental or emotional phenomenon and gives it an important role in his philosophy: namely, fear. What is this fear? We meet it as a phenomenon in the world and it has nothing to do with a power that resides over creation; nor is it a fear connected with some evil that menaces us. No, says Heidegger, it is occasioned by existence meeting itself as a slumbering possibility; for only existence itself can fear and feel anguish before itself. But what is it in existence that evokes fear and anguish? Heidegger's answer is that this anguish contains something of the sense of "not-to-be-at-home," *nicht Zuhause sein;* that is to say, a homelessness, a rootlessness.

Heidegger is well aware of this vulnerability. He proclaims a philosophical system in which there are no "safety nets." We can find no help outside of the world because our existence is exclusively an "existence within the world" *(in der Welt sein);* it is included implacably within the horizontality of the world outside of which we find only what Heidegger calls transcendent Being, which is by his definition inaccessible. Lacking any verticality and any superior element that could provide equilibrium in the world, existence is one-dimensional. The total subjectivity of man finds no objective points of support. It is therefore meaningless to try to find an explanation of the world, because our only option is to enter into existence. In a world so conceived, man is rootless and homeless, and Heidegger thus can add to his philosophy an extremely important psychic characteristic: The human condition involves anguish.

Time, as existential flux, is by no means a mechanical process. On the contrary, existence is "animated"; man enters a state of consciousness and the first thing he experiences is a clamorous calling *(Ruf)*. But this calling does not come from man himself, nor is it planned or desired. "Calling" expresses existence; this clamorous cry arises out of existence and has no message, no content. It is wordless, but at the same time, when considered by man, it is a dallying and an invitation to action, inviting us to go forth *(sich entwerfen)* in extroversion and to enter into all of the possibilities that the world offers. Man will be active; but when we understand the meaning of this calling (which has no meaning), we are, says Heidegger, conscious of anguish — and this, in more than a mere play on words, is the anguish of consciousness. We come to the horrible realization that anguish or dread is inherent in consciousness.

Heidegger sets consciousness before us, as it were, and his notion of "calling" *(Ruf)* is the voice of consciousness *(Stimme des Gewissens)*. Existence is speaking to itself — and

63

thereby to us — about this consciousness. Reception of this "calling" means that we are deployed in consciousness, that we understand ourselves; and when, volitionally, we accept this understanding, we enter into existence and into the possibilities that existence offers. But there is a very important consideration: Nothing could be further from the truth than to suppose that this consciousness is a guide toward the good and toward the elimination of the bad. To imagine that "I am good" is a Pharisaism, says Heidegger, because consciousness tells us merely that existence is calling to itself — and to us.

In consciousness we also encounter guilt; but we are not to regard guilt or consciousness as moral categories. Why not? Because guilt belongs to existence, it is a priori; existence is in debt to Being, and therefore existence bears the burden of guilt. At this point Heidegger introduces an upheaval of conventional ideas of morality and moral norms; or more precisely, he "delivers" existence from all moral substance. Conscience is nothing but the state of consciousness we gain when we listen to the existential *Ruf,* "calling." And we become aware of guilt when we are conscious of existence and of its debt to its own essence, Being.

What is truth? Even before Pilate, Aristotle posed this question; and his answer was the correspondence between the idea and the object of the idea, between knower and known. After a lapse of two thousand years, says Heidegger, we are still at this same point. His own answer is that truth is the discovery of existence itself. Man must discover what the world consists of, existence itself. And what we say about existence, this, too, is existence itself; for existence exhibits itself thereby. What we say about all of this with words, with our speech — this then will be truth.

This is total subjectivism speaking; truth is not something presupposed, assumed, or implied, because we are ourselves "in the truth." No distance exists between the ego and its object; everything is a subjective unity. Truth is nothing that has to be proven or demonstrated, nor can it be refuted. Existence itself is not something that can be subject to "proof." Truth can be seen and given names; but it is man who sees and who gives names; and it is man who sees and who gives names to truth, and he does this with words, by talking. This process of seeing and name-giving is what Heidegger calls truth. Speaking of "eternal truths" is nonsense, he says; this is only a remnant of Christian theological ideas, not yet radically expunged. The Philosopher of the City of Man has spoken.

VIII

Western secularization is at the threshold of its fulfillment, and Martin Heidegger provides the philosophical formulations for this decomposition. The world is one-dimensional, spatial, horizontal, endless. "Outside" of the sensory order are two pseudo-metaphysical notions: Being (as conceived by Heidegger) and Time. There are no higher powers, no higher values. To speak of such dualities as spirit and matter, good and evil, has no meaning; such ideas as grace, charity, mercy, and forgiveness are mere nonsense.

There is nothing immutable in Heidegger's worldview, and consequently there is no objectivity. The flow of time in which existence and hence man, too, are immersed can only be subjective, both conceptually and actually. Man himself must be regarded simply as a modality of this flat existence; and his consciousness is only what is afforded him by this existence. In this situation, the Gestalt that is man, with his durable and substantive character formed by centuries and centuries of Western thinking and by the sensitivities derived from this thought — all this counts for nothing and is completely denied. Further, the great paradox of Heidegger's philosophy is this: The grand picture of Western man, strong, free, conscious of his role, prepared to place himself on the throne of power, and lording it over all — all of this is now open to question. All ends in subjective dissolution wherein man himself loses all of his natural contours, all points of reference. A consequence without parallel in modern thinking is this: Heidegger makes the very conclusions of the secular conception of existence into a sensory stream, while at the same time providing the forms of consciousness that correspond to this description of reality. Heidegger's philosophy does not bring chaos; no, it provides a consciousness of this chaos and interprets it, thereby endorsing it. Herein is the great menace for the Western world.

Is it not necessary, or at least highly desirable, that the Christian world prepare for obligatory and unavoidable war in confronting existential philosophy? Not at all, or so it would seem; for we have seen only very weak and futile resistance mobilized by Christian theologians, custodians of the values of the West. In fact, most of Heidegger's ideas have been met with silence; and his philosophy is even regarded with positive interest and has been accepted and integrated into so-called existential theology.

In the modern West, theology has more and more taken on the character of pragmatism. Worldly and profane activity, social welfare, and profane ethical notions have increasingly thrust any lingering transcendence into the shadows. Objective, dogmatic systems of truth are replaced by subjective adventurism, not least on the level of social sentimentality. The spiritual loses its defining features, its contours obscured by a new emphasis on psychological speculations. From this point, it is but a short distance to the proclamations of the German theologian and existentialist Rudolf Bultmann: There is in man nothing that we can call a soul, nothing whereby man can find an exit from existence, nothing to justify the belief that man can throw himself into the arms of God, into eternity. Indeed, according to Bultmann, anyone who believes this will only throw himself into his own arms (*nur sich selbst in die Arme läuft*).

The blasphemers no longer have to scoff, for the ideas of sin and guilt have lost their lawfulness and force; nor do we have any more pardon and consolation. Theological disarmament has made significant contributions to this crisis. Its manifestations cannot be denied; there is crisis and confusion in our sense of identity.

The crisis of identity is twofold. First, it concerns the inner man who can no longer experience himself as a substantial unity, as a proud and self-conscious center of power — that great secular promise. But second, the crisis concerns our outer life as well: the dissolution of any normative social order and community, which are gradually replaced by an institutionalism governed from above by technocrats. We live in manifest and continuing crisis: Man is no longer en route to citizenship, but rather is on the way to becoming a new kind of passive subject in a helotism of the modern industrial and social state, with its technical perfection. And technical perfection logically means government from above. In the face of this technocratic hierarchy, every ideological system must experience its powerlessness.

The loss of the awareness of the ego, in the traditional understanding of the word, and the loss of a living, vital society — these constitute a double loss, the loss both of normative order and of community, both of which are essential for the wholeness of human life. A subsequent, further loss is that of stimulating ideals and goals. In this situation, the kernel of the crisis is a consciousness of emptiness; people yearn for a new content in their lives, something to fill the aching void. This is why the period between the two World Wars (the twenties and the thirties) sees the rise of reactionary and repressive movements, movements that are revolutionary but set before men a wonted opportunity to spend themselves in striving toward specific goals. These movements often win surprisingly large popular support. The regimes that result face outward toward what had been the Anglo-puritanical hope of 1919: "to make the world safe for democracy." These racist manifestations of force serve their purpose in the process of dissolution; but eventually the City of Man must declare war against these fantastic regimes with their one-party plebiscite "elections."

The Allied victory of 1945 is definitive, and not only over the fascist armies. It is much more significant that the victory in World War II is also a victory over and extirpation of the last remnants of traditional order in the Western world. The great victorious powers have affirmed that the unidimensionality of man is universally valid, and that the manner of life of the victors is exclusively right. Older, traditional forms for humane, social living in the West now belong to history; and as historical phenomena, they must be regarded as lower stages in the great tide of general human and social Progress.

This represents an exceedingly important change in the understanding of history. In his one-dimensionality, man now stands as dominant on earth, and the City of Man is the pseudo-metaphysical expression of this new order in the world. Existentially, this new order is without spatial or temporal boundaries; this is modernism. Finally, this new world order gives itself a political and doctrinal Gestalt: democracy.

In this "trinitarian" Gestalt — City of Man, modernism, and democracy — changes are implied in two essential ideas. First, in space there is no longer a genuine human or social identity; the new world order is a flux that banishes every stable point of reference, such points being essential for the establishment of any effective identity. Second, in time this new world order is ahistorical (or posthistorical). In its pseudo-metaphysical Gestalt, democracy is the City of Man; in its existential Gestalt, it is modernism. And democracy no longer has a historical role as a dynamic force negating traditionalism; it is the victory over the last antagonistic form of human social organization, to borrow an expression of Karl Marx. Democracy is now static, nonhistorical. It has no obligation, in the name of development, toward the future; nor does it any longer have any obligation toward the past.

But there is more to all of this. Democracy now becomes myth. It is Rousseau who at last wins a victory. It is his myth of sovereign Man, of the sovereign People, with its *Volonté Générale,* its General Will, that expresses what power is on the earth. Its primordial myth, resting in Nature's own bosom, is disclosed in the two "archetypes," liberty and equality. The myth must now confront the reality, and try to realize what the Jacobins could not. In virtue of its pseudo-original, mythical character, democracy has absolute validity in time and space; every alternative is excluded. In its myth of origin, democracy claims to represent an unchangeable order, invariable before every historical event and process, because it has its origin in Nature herself. This alleged supremacy of democracy first manifests itself when it gives a universal moral and judicial validity to the Nuremberg Tribunal.

IX

Traditionally, absolute and unrestricted liberty is reserved only for him who is above the entire universe and who is unfettered by anything in the created order, namely, Almighty God. But liberty is manifested on the terrestrial plane as well. In the Platonic sense, liberty is an archetype, a divine principle; consequently, earthly liberties are imperfect reflections of their celestial model and source. In the terrestrial order, the created is necessarily something incomplete, lacking full achievement, because it is bound to forms, limitations, and contradictions. Earthly liberties, therefore, though real in their own order, are inevitably conditional; they exist in the manner that freedom of movement exists within a labyrinth. But the democratic myth is one of absolute, total, and limitless liberty that believes it can marvelously change the world.

The states of liberty, on the one hand, and of constraint and lack of freedom, on the other, have both physical and psychological meanings. Our sense of living, that which we experience most inchoately and in a most primary sense, has self-assertion as a given, immanent force. For this reason, man has always been aware of liberty. We see liberty here in the aspect of contrast; it appears as the negation of power in all of its diversified forms — whether this power be other individuals, ethnic groups, or nations, or political, social, cultural, or ecclesiastical hierarchies. Liberty is an energy that always strives to deliver itself from structures and systems of order.

In historical development, therefore, liberty is a force that relativizes, corrects, dissolves, and sometimes revolutionizes. A healthy society is one that is capable of correcting its faults and renewing itself, and in this the desire for liberty has a very important role. The "progressive" forces of liberty are undoubtedly an important force in social life. But the apostles of absolute human liberty too easily forget two factors that are unavoidable limiting agents wherever liberty is concerned. First, profane existence is by no means immune from the menacing consequences of the audacious experiments undertaken in the desire for liberty. We often forget how fragile our social arrange-

70

ments in fact are, that we do not always have stable ground underfoot, and that the human individual is an everlasting well of energy. Belief in notions of unrestricted liberty have led liberal social movements into very ominous directions.

The second limiting factor concerns our possibilities of choice. Man has great possibilities of liberty: He can choose. His choice may concern some sensory object, or it may concern a system of norms or ethical ideas among which his conscience may decide; but he always has freedom of choice. In all of this we experience great freedom. It is very tempting to think that liberty is something endless, something without bounds; we are wont to think that, at long last, perhaps, we may be able to use liberty to escape the existential labyrinth.

We forget that when we have made a choice we are thereupon bound to the object of our choice. We live in a subject-object antinomy, and we cannot escape the antinomies of existence. Even freedom of will, freedom of choice, comes to an end, at least from the formal standpoint. We are bound to what we have freely chosen. If I may so express it, this is one of the paradoxes or absurdities of life.

We cannot deny that the desire for liberty has a positive value, and we must recognize its positive role in history. Both in individual and in social life the lack of human freedom would lead to stagnation and petrifaction. Life on earth is continuous change, a multiversum, and the element of human freedom is a necessary motive of action. In this sense, Norbert Wiener and Martin Heidegger are witnesses to truth.

But unbridled liberty has another aspect. It dissolves all ideas of value, it relativizes and atomizes. In the life of secularized man as well as in secularized society, strivings for liberty always open up new and growing sectors of pluralism and relativism at the expense of stability and continuity of values. Endless dialogue, debate, and scientific investigation fill the vacuum.

Medieval Ockhamist nominalism dissolved the ideas and values formed and molded in Christian experience, transforming these into an atomism of thought and ideas under the seal of freedom of thought. Similarly, Western profane science cultivates a method of structural analysis that leads to excellent scientific achievements, but at the same time leads to atomization, separativity, and definitely not — be it noted — to what was the early dream of profane science, namely a great synthesis of the knowledge of existence. The inverting and revolutionary effects of liberty are evident especially in aesthetics. When the plastic arts as well as poetry and music become areas of aesthetic experimentation, the values of beauty as invariable states and forms of consciousness are more and more dissolved, so that in the end there is nothing left to "revolutionize." The final result is that the aesthetic negates itself; art exhibits itself as "anti-art."

Liberty, in its aspect of a relativizing, atomizing force, one that dissolves all values — we speak still of liberty as an element in historical processes — leads to a state of pluralism that is then invoked as one of the noble, indispensable fruits of Western development and modern life. We see the advent of the heterodox and of so-called tolerance. Heterodoxy not only strives toward moral and theological "liberalization," but also toward emancipation from axiomatic truths inherent deep in nature herself (and, notably, human nature), from what is traditionally held to be the natural order. We cannot forget that every human being and every society has, and must have, taboos — instinctive prejudices,[1] if you will — that are neces-

1. *Prejudice* obviously has its negative connotations; but too often we overlook that the word can convey something eminently positive, namely, a synthetic and axiomatic apprehension of normal limits. As such, prejudice is a preternatural and protective judgment — and a psychological instrument that is employed by liberals fully as much as by anyone else.

sary for its very existence. Western liberalism is a historical process that, linked with heterodoxy in the name of liberty, continuously attacks these forms of order. And this is one of the most effective ways to disarm and destroy a society: take from it its very possibilities of self-defense.

The struggle against physical and mental oppression has often been a positive element in Western development. The shadow side of this, however, the other side of the coin, is the disastrous dissolution of values, even of the very idea of value, of normative systems, of the taboos and prejudices necessary to personal as well as to social life — a dissolution sanctioned by a misconceived liberty. And now, when liberty is proclaimed to have the status of myth and is thereby thrust forward with demands that it be absolute, total, and without limits — in this we see that the myth of liberty becomes anarchy.

The "virtual" aspect of heterodoxy is so-called tolerance. In its Voltairian sense, tolerance is announced as the noble hallmark of Western freedom, and is contrasted with orthodox intransigence. But Voltaire, in his hatred of orthodoxy, has distorted the picture. The essential meaning of the word *tolerance* is forbearing and patient endurance; historically, it means an appeal to magnanimity, and evenhandedness toward people of different opinions. Tolerance does not mean the surrender of truth nor of one's own positions; nor does it imply passivity or "brotherly love" when a valid system of values is reduced to ashes. Respect for one's fellow beings is immanent in tolerance; and this implies recognition of one's own and one's fellow's imperfection as well as worth.

From the historical perspective, tolerance is always subject to tests; it is something that is always wrestling with limits. Where, indeed, are the limits of tolerance, of patience? Tolerance loses its meaning when it is not linked with compassion, with *caritas*, which clearly implies not only self-knowledge but

73

also knowledge of human nature. When tolerance is reduced to the mere expression of the general liberal denial of values, it is no longer, as it is claimed to be, an expression of humane sentiments and love for mankind. Having reached this point, "tolerance" has lost all meaning and is merely an expression of indifference. It is then only a short way to the demand for a war of extermination against the traditional, the qualitative, the orthodox, the venerable. *Ecrasez l'infame,* said Voltaire.

Liberty is one of the foundation stones of the democratic myth. In the historical process, liberty was a notion of contrast and a necessary element in the struggle against oppression and enslavement. Liberty is a necessary element in a vital society, an essential factor that brings equilibrium to earthly life. But in the democratic myth as it has been proclaimed since the Second World War, liberty no longer has this mission. In the contemporary one-dimensional world, it is elevated into something that is principial, absolute, boundless, nonhistorical, and that requires no qualification.

We are only too well aware that after the heady days of victory in 1945, harmony has not entered the world; quite to the contrary, new controversies, new moral and mental problems, have arisen; new phenomena of disequilibrium have been manifested. In politics and administration, in ethics and jurisprudence, order and the very idea of order are being denied and more and more thrust aside. Man and society in the Western world are in accelerating decay and face the gravest functional problems. Why? Liberty is now regarded as an "archetypal" totality and consequently has been made into something unlimited that cannot be reined in. The gates of dissolution and decomposition have been opened, and a low and blind pragmatism beckons. Everything that can be experienced is permitted, according to Gottfried Benn. When liberty continuously oversteps all boundaries, we must ask whether these trespasses can ever stop short of lies, of error for error's sake, the most flagrant abuses. An answer comes from Jean d'Ormession: If you deny liberty to those who are mistaken, then there is no more liberty; because to defend liberty is to defend its misuses. *(Si vous refusez la liberté à ceux qui se trompent, il n'y a plus de liberté. Défendre la liberté, c'est defendre ses abuses).*

At last, high above all time and space, absolute liberty becomes a narcissistic ego-manifestation; a way of behavior in which man, however weak he may be in his ego-consciousness, can regard himself as in a mirror and see himself as the carrier of all physical and mental energies to which he thinks his total liberty entitles him.

X

The victors of 1945 have the task of preparing the way for the everlasting state whose enemies must be extirpated, even in a principial sense. The hierarchical, authoritarian forces, last remnants of the traditional order, must now be replaced by a one-dimensional, democratic value system. In the name of tolerance and liberty, therefore, a surgical excision has to be performed; an excision that has its moral and judicial sanction from a universally valid triumph before which the defeated enemy and his deeds, the war crimes, are to be condemned in the name of humanity. But is this enough?

It is not enough that victory will result in an enduring state; nor is it enough to proclaim liberty as a narcissistic manifestation of the ego. The democratic myth has another foundation stone, necessary to guarantee this victory: equality. If democracy will make the coming *saturnalia* durable, it must display itself as an order, an order that is sacrosanct. Equality will render this possible.

It is said that before the divine, there are no differences between men; but this is true only in the sense that the Creator has given to every man an inner, immortal Light. In this Light we are conscious of the Divine Reality ("In thy light shall we see light"; Ps. 36:9, KJV). And therefore we can have a creed and be confident that God will save us. The Creator has given us value and dignity, making us equal in his eye in this respect. But this equality is spiritual; in its terrestrial manifestation it is qualitative, and thus essentially different from the ambitions of the City of Man to establish an equality of a purely quantitative kind.

History is full of fraternal battles, and we ceaselessly confront brutality and intolerance, the desire for power and the desire for revenge. Man represses and will be repressed; he persecutes and will be persecuted. When the repressed and the persecuted rise up in revolt it is not necessarily and simply from base motives of revenge. In such cases we can share with the revolutionaries a deep thirst for justice and dignity; and it is true that demands for equality are often made in such situations. Equality, like liberty, is an idea of contrast; the legitimate desire for equality reflects a need to reestablish a reasonable order while eliminating unreasonable and intolerable arrangements. In this sense, equality is, in the historical process, a positive ambition to restore a proper balance in the relations between human beings and societies. Equality is an effort to limit and as far as possible to eliminate the "law of the jungle," and we can successfully pursue these aims by legislation and by the administration of justice. In the historical perspective, equality is the endeavor to achieve peace and harmony in earthly life.

But in the utopian dream world, equality has a different function and position. When everyone is on the same level, when everyone receives exactly the same portion of what life has to offer, say the utopians, then peace and harmony will dominate and human fraternity will become a reality. Tales and dreams; utopias have been cultivated for millennia, but until recently they have always had a subordinate position as compared with social realities. It is only in our own time, when the great myth of democracy makes its entry and when equality is established as a pseudo-archetype, an essential element in this system, that fable and reality change positions. Equality is no longer merely a subordinate element in our mental and biological actuality, in the created and natural world; it is now heralded as absolute and integral, an "archetypal" foundation stone in the City of Man.

Consequently, with the modern demand for equality, all that is hierarchical in the natural order of creation is in principle denied. It is probably impossible to say definitively to what extent interference in the basic biological structures of ordinary life is possible; and the same is true for our mental capacities. But there are three sectors of our existence in which it is easy to see how ambitions have expanded and changed the conditions of human life when compared with traditional social orders. These three sectors are: relations between the sexes; relations between adults and children; and relations between different ethnic groups.

The so-called feminist emancipation in Western countries has a long history, and it essentially concerns accommodations and changes in technology and society, changes that have deeply affected traditional patterns and conditions of life, especially in the family and in the professions. Thoroughgoing accommodations in feminine life have become more or less imperative. What has been decisive in principle, however, especially in these last decades in the West, has been the tendency to level out, even to efface the very differences between the sexes. And therewith inevitably come conflicts, not only between the sexes but even within both sexes themselves.

Following Rousseau, relations between adults and children have also entered a new phase. Rousseau's tale of little Emile was, so to speak, a pedagogical sleeping beauty for two centuries; but recently, after World War II, his ideas — until now cultivated only by pedagogical extremists — have become widespread; and pretentious plans are being laid for new relationships between adult and child, between the ripe and the unripe. Democratic extremists now proclaim that pedagogical life will become an integral administration in the name of equality, already established in the workplace. It will be realized in conformity with the romantic, idyllic atmosphere of Rousseau's Nature and the comradeship established between little Emile and his older pedagogical friend, Jean-Jacques, on the Savoyard farm.

All of these pedagogical fantasies, introducing a premature citizenship in the schoolyard, cannot of course stand up to brutal reality. Nevertheless, we must be aware that the notion of eliminating all differences between the mature and the immature has already made great progress. Not least in this field is the fact that in Sweden, children have won a "status of justice" that puts definite limits on how adults can discipline and nurture children.

World War II brought important changes in relations between the peoples of the earth. It marks an end to the colonial systems, understood in the conventional sense. It also marks the beginning of open and unrestricted communication between the peoples of the world. Thousands of years of traditions formed in the matrix of ethnic and racial idiosyncrasies are thrust into the background; the dominant idea is that man is a universal creature formed by democratic egalitarianism. New institutions, new ethnic and aesthetic forms, and new political and social ideologies are implanted throughout the world — manifestations of Western imperialism more effective and far-reaching than the older colonialisms ever were.

The great hope in the Western world is that when all of the peoples of the world meet in an atmosphere of democratic egalitarianism there will be peace. Humanity will at long last realize the dream of 1789. This dream also has an element of hope: Common life will engender a kind of symbiosis, though just where the parameters of this symbiotic process are to be found is not clearly expressed. What is undeniable today is that instincts of preservation must be overcome and assigned to lower, "barbaric" periods. Modern man must be delivered from all forms of "prejudice."

Struggles for equality are often of value; they motivate and are even necessary for much in the human community as seen from the historical perspective. This much is undeniable. But equality as an integral, absolute foundation of society, as it is represented in the democratic myth, is something else altogether. Conceived in this way, equality is a denial of God's created order and also of the natural order, both of which have horizontal as well as vertical dimensions. Mankind is polarized into two sexes, and man and woman have distinct but complementary biological and psychological characteristics[2] that cannot be annihilated without nefarious consequences. A human life is a process of maturation,[3] and this life process does not admit that men and women, nor adults and children, are equivalent. A people, a nation, has an identity deeply rooted in its history, its language, its culture, its life forms — good and bad — and this community must be defended. What we call identity is always on guard against the cosmopolitan dissolution of norms. It is also, as Ernest Renan said, a spiritual principle: *une ame, un principe spirituel*.

2. The fact that it is necessary to call attention to these elementary truths indicates the extent of our cultural decay.
3. "Men must endure their going hence, even as their coming hither; ripeness is all" (*King Lear* v.ii.9).

Egalitarianism, in its modern absolutist form, attacks the divine order of creation, and it does so not only as a denial and repudiation of this order in its endless nuanced multiformity. In addition, the City of Man demands a conformity in the widest sense of that word. The earth is populated by billions of men and women, and these human masses represent endless individual differences in bodily characteristics, in temperament, in intelligence, and in spiritual and cultural practices. But this diversity cannot be permitted in the City of Man, where power and sovereignty rest not so much in the hands of the individual as in what is called the people, humanity, mankind. Sovereign Man cannot reveal himself in such a diversified, manifold unfolding. The higher, "divine" spectacle of man would not then be trustworthy.

This is the pressure to conform that de Tocqueville observed during his renowned visit to the United States in the 1820s. But here we note that not only can we regard as twins the two "archetypes" — liberty and equality — of the democratic myth, but that they also exhibit a fundamental contradiction. Liberty is intrinsically nonconformist; it is bound to the ego both in its physical and psychic aspects. In its more passionate forms, liberty expresses a refractory narcissism. But in its essence, liberty is qualitative.

Modernist equality, on the contrary, is conformist; it lacks quality because it is essentially quantitative, and its goal is to dominate and to establish an order. Egalitarianism is arithmetic; it can be realized statistically and can establish control and govern from central points of command. Equality subjugates, but liberty proclaims its invincibility.

If the democratic myth were only a proclamation of liberty, the whole democratic construction, the whole edifice, would be thrown out of balance and anarchy would result. Liberty, the fight for freedom, is an ego-exaltation that gives man the possibility to exhibit his egoistic nakedness; therefore equality is a necessary counterbalance. But at the same time, equality is a menace for liberty; it can become a means of oppression in the hands of a central authority. When liberty and equality meet, therefore, conflict is unavoidable. This inner, immanent contradiction exists in democracy. Who is winning, and who is losing? When egalitarian demands for order and conformity gain the upper hand, what can the subtle and "aristocratic" values of liberty offer by way of resistance? In the one-dimensional City of Man, equality dominates the landscape.

Liberty has a psychic foundation: narcissism. Equality also has a psychic foundation, but one that is more exterior and more ignoble: namely, resentment, the indefatigable struggle to undermine and bring down the superior, the strong, the high-minded, to gain power and influence by winning ascendancy for the inferior; and this is a potent weapon within democracy. An additional consideration is that resentment finds something lacking to liberty, namely, an additional source of moral energy. For equality always marches in lockstep with the notion of justice, even if the notion be erroneously conceived.

Equality produces and continuously mobilizes moral energies. It is not difficult to understand what this moral "production" means for the democratic myth. This egalitarian morality has a double effect; it is simultaneously camouflage and manipulation. Egalitarian resentment and collective egoism are draped in moral elevation; individual and collective egoism are elevated to the level of moral dignity. The democratic myth can be proclaimed in very good conscience.

This moral system, however, is vulnerable. It is bound to earthly life and can certainly be the object of critical discrimination and analysis, of doubt and attack. One can assault a profane and egalitarian system of order, even if it is presented as moral. But democracy is not only a system of earthly morality; it is something more, and in this "something more" equality finds its way to triumph: equality is righteousness. Equality raises us to a pseudo-metaphysical level where democracy and all it stands for are absolute, total, and boundless. In this world, Man is the vehicle for this righteousness; and in the name of righteousness, Man can proclaim himself as the legitimate, sovereign possessor of all that we regard as terrestrial power.

XI

In the edifice of the democratic myth, something is still lacking. To liberty and equality we must add a third element: power. In the traditional order, the source of power is God, the Almighty. In him, power resides in its essence; all other power is derived from this essential power. God manifests himself in the creative process, if we may speak thus. Power in its essence is one and indivisible; but as an element in creation, power is seen as a duality: the possessor of power, and the object toward which power is directed.

Power and the exercise of power as elements of the world are manifested in innumerable areas and in innumerable forms. It is to be found wherever organic life is found. Without power, nature would be delivered up to boundless chaos. We encounter power in cooperation, in struggle, as structure, and in hierarchy. We also encounter power and its exercise in human, civilized co-existence. Constitutionally, power is delegated by the Creator to human beings; and this is expressed symbolically and most lucidly in the traditional monarchical order where the king governs "by the grace of God" and is responsible before his celestial Principle.

The traditional idea of power means, therefore, that in the first place all power derives from essential power, that is, the divine Source of power; second, that the world is the field of manifestation of power; and third, that this power in its worldly, dualistic forms is nevertheless linked to essential power that flows from its divine Source. Divinity, therefore, is also in the world as judicial essence. In this we have the foundation for worldly power, and from this foundation we experience worldly power as authority, *auctoritas*. When we speak of the exercise of earthly power as erecting structures and creating order, as binding and commanding, as limiting and dominating, it is first of all not a question of the possession or usurpation of power in the physical sense, implying that a stronger suppresses a weaker. Terrestrial power has a qualitative content before all else, and this is because of the Source of its derivation. Nothing that can be said of the brutal misuses of power that fill the history of mankind can contradict this; it only confirms the imperfection of everything earthly.

In the West, the medieval period is full of conflicts revolving around the primacy of the spiritual authority and the exercise of secular power. In the baroque states, debates about human nature are deeply involved in questions concerning the source of power. As secularist conceptions of earthly existence advance, power is regarded as a "contract" between the dominating and the dominated. But a duality remains, and Rousseau is the first artificially to separate the problem from all contact with reality. His solution is a fantastic and facile manipulation: everyone exercises tyranny over everyone else.

And this is a real revolution in human thinking regarding power. Rousseau proclaims that in its earthly manifestation, power is no longer to be regarded as a structural, binding, and hierarchical duality. Existence, and hence power, is one-dimensional. Power, in its earthly condition consisting of divided sectors, is no more. Thousands of years of the expression of power, manifesting a spiritual and qualitative mission, *auctoritas,* is nothing else for Rousseau than the domination of the stronger, and this domination is essentially physical. *La force est une puissance physique.* No authority deriving from the divine Source is to be found in Rousseau's one-dimensional system. The history of mankind, he says, is the history of flagrant injustice. He therefore begins his work on the social contract *(Contrat social)* with the words: *L'homme est né libre et partout il est dans les fers* — man is born free and everywhere he is in chains.

I repeat: This a revolution in human thinking. Rousseau here provides the philosophical foundation for Karl Marx. Power no longer has a higher source; it is now only physical. The qualitative has been replaced by the quantitative. Mankind is divided into two groups, the dominating and the dominated. But all of this will now be changed. Political power is placed in the hands of the people; all men are citizens, and they vote. Power is numerical, statistical; the many are stronger than the few.

Does this mean that Rousseau has formulated a cynical theory of power, delivering mankind up to oppression in new and exquisite forms? No, indeed. According to Rousseau, the Social Contract brings men together, expressing something beyond individual interests. The Social Contract has an "essence," and in understanding that essence mankind unites personally with its energies in that "higher" meaning of citizenship — *la volonté générale,* the Popular Will.

With the Popular Will, Rousseau completes his edifice, the democratic myth; this myth is brought to the fore by the men of 1945. Without this "higher will," neither liberty nor equality is enough to erect the edifice of democracy. With the *volonté générale,* the people now have the means for auto-coronation; now they win a pseudo-metaphysical exaltation. The people "divinize" themselves. Now the pressure for self-worship can be acknowledged; now the golden calf can be brought out.

Rousseau adds something else to this "divinization": the will of the people invigorates. Popular power is, indeed, an unchangeable and exalted order, and the myth is in itself invincible. But the myth must give dynamism to the people, driving them to act, to change, to achieve. The people must "will" something. The democratic myth has a necessary postulate: that we have a dynamism, that man in his individual as well as in his collective form must will something with his power.

In the final analysis, what is it that we call popular, democratic power? Beyond the expressed will of the people, as it is supposedly formulated, there is no appeal; here we met the absolute, the universal, the indivisible, and the immovable. There is nothing a priori, nothing anterior to democratic power; no ideas of truth, no notions of good or bad, can bind the Popular Will. This "will" is free in the sense that it stands above all notions of value. It is egalitarian because it is reared on arithmetic equality. In the traditional order, there was a qualitative duality, because there was a divine Source of power, a higher Will that always allowed room for forgiveness, consolation, charity. The Popular Will knows none of this; its sentences are implacable. It is not open to any appeal, it listens to no demand for grace, no plea for compassion. Like the Sphinx, the Popular Will is immovable in its enigmatic silence.

The democratic myth is now complete in its sham "trinitarian" unity. Mankind is free, equal, and almighty. Man lives in a one-dimensional world, under nothing superior. In this liberty, he can now exhibit his narcissism; in his equality, he finds his earthly moral justice; and in his power, he finds his "divine" perpetuity. What the Jacobins of 1789 proclaimed but could not realize is now preached by the men of 1945 and those who follow. The myth, now that all ideological fires are extinct, will compensate for the threat of emptiness. The two "archetypes," liberty and equality, provide man his ego-manifestation and his moral legitimation; and in the Popular Will he discovers himself as a higher being, individually as well as collectively. He is the bearer of all earthly power.

But the myth must now confront reality. Man now faces the world as the self-governing being that he believes himself to be, swollen with pride and afloat in ignorant self-esteem. No one can accuse, bring to trial, or judge a sovereign. Man is his own legislator; and as Rousseau emphasizes, what is highest is not the law but the legislating, the law-giving will. And this law-giving will belongs to the subject, sovereign man. The logical conclusion can only be that man is without guilt, without sin; and what has been expressed as worship in the Christian sacrifice will now be replaced, in the democratic myth, by an existential guiltlessness.

In the traditional order, an autocratic monarch could become a tyrant, repressing and obliterating all of his antagonists; but even a tyrant could be called to account for his crimes and for the violation of his solemn responsibilities. Even a tyrant lives and rules in a qualitative duality; there were always forces, always men who could assume responsibility and overthrow and displace him. The democratic myth effaces objectivity and duality; this is what it means to live in universal subjectivity, in a noncontradictory seclusion.

When secularized man confronts this solitary subjectivity, a crisis arises. Man meets himself, and no one can be unconscious of the limits of human capacity. Even if the City of Man denies this, the consciousness of guilt nevertheless exists as an element in human self-awareness. Heidegger tries to explain it, but he does not deny it. This consciousness does not diminish; rather, it is increasing because secularized man lacks something of great value that traditional man possessed: the possibility of forgiveness, of grace and *caritas*. Absolutized democracy closes the door on this way of transcendence and egress.

Man must now confront his guilt. Now begins what Kafka called the Process. Now the great philosopher of the City of Man, Martin Heidegger, confirms that the existential stream of time includes guilt and that man is necessarily involved with fear and anxiety. But does not modern man have a great compensation in citizenship? Is not citizenship the great human assumption of responsibility and social morality?

Actually, the father of universal citizenship, Jean-Jacques Rousseau, has abolished the foundations of this citizenship because he proclaims the unidimensionality of popular sovereignty. For Rousseau, the highest norm is not law; the highest norm is the will of man, above which nothing can be admitted. But genuine citizenship is realized only on condition that man accepts an order of virtue that is superior to him, which is expressed as a manifestation of heavenly norms and of heavenly power over him. Unidimensionality annihilates the possibility of virtue.

The concept of citizenship, in aristocratic times, was a fascinating ideal and goal. Today, when men live as if in a hall of mirrors and in subjectivist seduction, they behave as de Tocqueville observed during his American tour: Nowhere is man so insignificant as in a democracy. Democratic man flatters himself, but he cannot shut out an awareness of his real situation. He has placed himself squarely within the process of secularization, and must recognize that now he is nothing more than the sum of psycho-physical functions in the universal existential flux, in effect nothing more than a welter of chaotic and fleeting sensory impressions.

Democratic man cannot escape the experience of powerlessness. It is a curious fact that nothing makes democratic man so confused, even irritated, as calling his attention to the enormous power that he is said to possess. He does not deny the principle of popular sovereignty, but it lurks in the shadows as a kind of half-conscious power held in reserve, one that we are supposed to bring out into the light and defend when authoritarian dangers threaten. On such occasions, one observes a state of excitement, of collective narcissism. But this reaction must be seen as a means of self-assurance and not at all as an expression of a consciousness of dignity and power.

Concealing, veiling, or maneuvering around the sense of powerlessness is commonly accomplished through escapism, and the avenues of escape are basically two. Sancho Panza is the classical literary figure illustrating one of these. His master, Don Quixote, has promised the little squire that he will be made governor of an island, but if he should find the power and responsibility too onerous, he can always find an exit: He can lease it out. And Cervantes lets the reader know that when Sancho Panza finally finds that his governorship is in fact too heavy for him, he is overtaken by real fear; and with deep gratitude he returns to reality and to his simple role as servant.

Sancho Panza returns to private life; countless are the multitudes of men who go the same way. Private life is found to be the great territory for escape, where man can rest and be delivered from the yoke of almighty democracy. The modern social state helps, offering excellent possibilities and all of the needed guarantees of welfare and security, that umbrella under which private man can live. Even Marxist-Leninist systems led to the paradoxical situation of the great mass of inhabitants, "Soviet man," striving more and more for purely private interests under a growing, flourishing power of peoples' commissars.

The retreat into private life is one of the main avenues of escapism; it is the passive expression of the experience of powerlessness. But another way of escapism expresses a more active and compensatory attitude: this is when people experience great democratic leadership, the charismatic aspect of the democratic myth. Powerlessness is never better concealed than when people place themselves in the shadow of a great leader, those momentous personas with whom the people can identify. There are almost no limits to the generosity and the hopes — but also to the deceptions — that the democratic masses invest in their leaders, their father figures. The self-esteem of the masses is here raised to sublime heights. If the possibilities of identification between the leaders and their followers are sufficiently strong, then every feeling of powerlessness is obliterated. Moreover, the notion of popular sovereignty is never undermined for these adorers, even when confronted with confessions of deception and failure from the master himself. Jean-Jacques Rousseau, in a frank declaration about the Social Contract, wrote that a real democracy has never existed and will never exist, because such a state of affairs is against the order of nature. The great mass of men can never bear the governing power. *Il n'a jamais existé de véritable démocratie, et il n'en existera jamais. . . . Il est contra l'ordre naturel que la grande nombre gouverne.* In this fit of candor, Rousseau was in full accord with the Scholastic adage that *nihil agit in seipsum,* nothing acts upon itself.

In democratic leadership we see manipulation and the psychological phenomenon of projection at the highest level. The leader will be the incarnation of the *volonté générale,* the bearer and executor of what is said to be the people's inner "will." These strong and charismatic leading figures are the magnified images of what the masses want to be themselves. The leader is the "mirror" delivering man from perceptions of his own powerlessness and insignificance; he is the father figure, giving to his adherents what they believe is the real Popular Will.

XII

The outcome of the Second World War is not only a military victory in the conventional sense; it is also a victory in an inner sense. Mankind is confronted with good and bad; with a choice between Fascism, which is bad, and the order proclaimed by the victors, which is, by definition, good. This proclamation itself has a more interior meaning: the denial in principle and the annihilation of the traditional order. It means the denial of more than a thousand years of energy directed toward moral and spiritual ends, the inner content of the traditional. Ideologically expressed, it means the annihilation of conservatism.

The dispositions that found expression in the proclamation of victory in 1945 can also be expressed in "trinitarian" terms: the City of Man, modernism, democracy. The City of Man affirms the omnipotence that free and equal man, in his endless one-dimensionality, has granted to himself — to deny or to doubt, which is blasphemy. No longer can any higher power set limits to human omnipotence; no responsibility need be vindicated for transgressing any borders; for, *mirabile dictu*, there are no longer any borders. The City of Man is total godlessness; it is the pseudo-metaphysical dimension of this "trinity."

The world, dominated by man, everlasting in time and endless in space, is an existential flux without origin and without goal. For man nothing else is left but to be identical — with himself. Willy-nilly, whether he intends it or not, he is enclosing himself within an autism of his own making. He can no longer surpass himself, no longer pass out of the prison of his ego. His own prisoner, he finds compensation in the narcissistic reflected images of himself and of his idols. In a subjectivism that is without horizons and timeless, he can no longer give an objective answer to his own questions. If he asks questions, he is only throwing himself into his own arms, as the existentialist theologian Bultmann said. In this state, when the historical also loses its meaning, we encounter the existential dimension of this unholy "trinity": modernism.

How is omnipotent man using his power in his City? In this existential flux, there are no stable points, no supports; the absolute is replaced by the relative, the qualitative is replaced by the quantitative. In the art of governing, man has a new means of administration: statistics; and a means of power: voting. The world is placed, willy-nilly, under a principle of power. More implacable than God's will under a millennial creed is the present domination of the majority over the minority. For God's will was always linked with *caritas*, with forgiveness, grace, and compassion. The will of the majority, on the contrary, is unconditional; it requires unconditional surrender. To the pseudo-metaphysical dimension of this "trinity," the City of Man, and to its existential dimension, modernism, we must now add a third: naked political and physical power — democracy. For in this modernistic, democratic City of Man, we must vote on everything, even on virtue[4] and righteousness. And what then of the righteous minorities?

4. "In the fatness of these pursy times, virtue itself of vice must pardon beg" (*Hamlet* III.iv.153).

The Ideology of Socialism

Large-scale industrialism and commercialism mark a total change of orientation in human social life. The world of freedom that socialism promised man is gravely threatened by these dynamisms, the effect of which is to destroy the balance and harmony that the liberals thought were at hand. Industrialism and commercialism call into existence a new, rapidly developing, and unstable social class, the proletariat. This new class challenges all that liberalism has disseminated, a challenge that is in the first instance mental. Notwithstanding all of the shortcomings and misery that accompanied it, the old paternalism, linked so closely with agriculture and handicraft, at least provided the worker with some semblance of fatherhood and a measure of protection and mercy. In the world of industrial and commercial gigantism, however, there could be no room for paternal care. The vertical element in the traditional social order was thoroughly eroded and then replaced by the industrial system. A new power structure, that of capitalism, takes the place of the old social arrangements. A new class of wageworkers, fatherless and embittered in their sense of impotence, seeks a new route: that of brotherhood.

Gradually, a new teaching emphasizing equality confronts the priority that liberalism gives to freedom. Instead of liberalism's social atomism, self-assertion, and competition, the new teaching enjoins collectivism, solidarity, and cooperation. An inner contradiction is unmasked in the industrial order: collective production versus private ownership, a new form of production that implies cooperation over against ownership by and in the interest of a minority. The new social class of proletarians, fatherless and unpropertied, turns with rising anger against this system and demands that it be changed. It is true that early in the nineteenth century the so-called Luddites of England believed that the solution lay in destroying all of the machinery and technical equipment in the factories. But this was only a very brief episode, and we soon witness the birth of movements that on the one hand affirm the industrial order, and on the other hand fiercely demand that collective ownership be added to the already collective form of production.

We have here an entirely new teaching, and when it is given the name "socialism" we have the key to its origin as a mental construct. At this point a vacuum obviously opens in the entire process of social development in the West. The liberal promise of a world of freedom, progress, and sensual pleasure proves to be something only for the very few. In turn, the new social class of the industrial proletariat rejects the arrangements of individualization and atomization. This new social class does not seek its sense of identity in its own selfhood; rather, it pursues security by inventing a substitute for the lost sense of fatherhood. But security is vital, and the new working class seeks to guarantee this need through an immediate, secular sense of brotherhood, a community molded in the forms of solidarity and collectivism.

Socialism as an ideology indeed results from the consciousness of deprivation, from the sense of a lost paternal function, from a lost sense of fatherhood, the sense of a social vacuum, and the awareness of a society based on liberal competition. The socialist answer to this loss is brotherhood and mutual solidarity, in order to put an end to competition. Logically, this leads to various notions of shared ownership, thereby disclosing the central idea of socialism in all its many varieties. But how shall one achieve the practical route to all of this immense social change, and what will be the final form of the socialist state?

Around the middle of the nineteenth century a series of disparate socialist teachings arrive on the scene, involving the most varied programs and promises. Most of these theories are now no more than curiosities on the dusty shelves of ideological history. Would the exciting new mental horizons of socialism have garnered any meaningful significance from the theoretical world of a Cabet? From the experiment in public manufacturing drawn up by Louis Blanc? From the socio-ethical romanticism of Pierre Leroux, or the concupiscent barrack life of Charles Fournier? Or in the anarchic world of Pierre-Joseph Proudhon, with its free associations and exchange banks under the eyes of the goddess Justicia? If all of these fantasies had been destined to be the mental nourishment of socialist and communist theoreticians throughout the world, this global movement would have found itself in a state of incessant confusion, halt and impotent while endeavoring to elaborate its socialist paradigms. The powerful ideological stream that flows through the nineteenth and well into the twentieth centuries thrives basically on Marxism, as does the broad social movement that has gathered millions and millions of supporters under the red banners.

All of the previous socialist movements tied themselves to a static order, as a function of their theoretical models. Karl Marx, however, radically breaks with this speculative and, as he contemptuously calls it, "Utopian" mode of thought. Instead, he presents his teaching as a science. And this alleged science

94

is not merely a teaching on the "hows" and "whys" of the world, but also about how the world must be changed and about the ways these changes are to be accomplished. To use Marx's own words, he teaches "a science of the conditions for the liberation of the working class." Marx puts this ideological complex in a dynamic form that deals with order in a world dominated by capitalism and industrialism; and he does so by presenting his ideas as a science and a philosophy of history.

Scientifically, Marx fundamentally aligns himself with British political economy; he adopts David Ricardo's theory of value, but he adds the concept of "surplus value." That is, in the process of capitalistic production the worker is transformed into a good, a commodity. The unpropertied proletarian sells his labor to the capitalist, Marx says, and the salary corresponds to the average production and reproduction of the labor force — that is, the vital sustenance that is necessary for the worker. The proletarian worker creates infinitely more, however, than the value received in wages or salary; and apart from that portion of the profit which is used to cover costs of production and for enlarging the factory and investments, there arise enormous new riches that Marx describes as surplus. This notion of surplus value is a cornerstone in the Marxist doctrinal system because it expresses not only a scientific truth but the fundamental moral injustice under which the productive class, the proletariat, is excluded from the very values that it creates.

Here we find the source of the slave rebellion that Marx himself proclaims. This implacable rebellion, this class struggle, rests on a firm scientific basis, Marx tells us; namely, surplus value as a fact of political economy. At the same time, this teaching lays bare a deeply unjust order: The proletariat is the object of exploitation, extortion, and alienation (*Entäusserung*). This science of the liberation of the working class also bears a moral message, one that is universal in character. Marx manages to "inflame" scientific ambition and to assimilate this into his new order. Marxism is not only a rational and scientific system, it also comprises an ethical message.

All other socialistic systems lacked ideological dynamism, but Marx manages to infuse this into his teachings by combining a scientific theory and a moral imperative. Surplus value infringes on human dignity, so we must extirpate this infringement from the world. No compromises are possible. The irreconcilable character of the class struggle emanates from the ethical significance of the surplus value theory. We have here a kind of Fall of Man that can be harmonized only by the literal eradication of the offending system. Every compromise, every "reformistic" solution, is excluded; and when Marx is reminded that some manual laborers are reasonably well paid, he dismisses this fact by calling them "better salaried slaves" (besser salarierte Sklaven).

What then? Will the coming upheaval be like another blind Spartacus rebellion? No, by no means. Marxism is a science, but it is also a philosophy of history. The ruling ideology of the dominant third estate, the middle class, is liberalism. Its philosophical basis is positivism. The proclaimed goal of this ideology is, in turn, the achievement of steadily expanding freedom that will guarantee uninterrupted progress. The concept of progress involves the wish and the effort to eliminate the dialectical character of life; this shall be done by empirical, analytical, and positivistic methods. As a method of attaining truth, positivism presupposes that the theory of knowledge involved is individualistic, and that the method of investigation shall be entirely unfettered so that truth and righteousness can be achieved as final goals of the investigative process.

The positivistic attitude excludes existential and logical opposites such as truth-falsehood or just-unjust. This is where dialectic enters the picture. Is it not possible, dialectic asks,

96

that a *tertium quid* or third factor can be perceived as included in such opposites, and that this third factor can finally emerge through the fruitful struggle of the opposites? Contradiction, dialectic holds, is the center point of life. These are the opposites that support life. They form the dynamic source of movement in all natural, human, and historical processes. Marxian dialectic asks, therefore, why there must always exist — as positivism argues — causal relationships. This is as if to ask, Why cannot something be simultaneously itself and its opposite?

Karl Marx is a dialectician, and through dialectics he attacks bourgeois-liberal positivism. The hope nourished by positivism is that man shall prove himself able to eliminate life's dialectical stratagems. Through logical-discursive processes life will be able to distinguish truth from falsity, and this will open the way to noncontradictory statements. By means of such structural analyses, man is able to gain knowledge of causal laws and ultimately will become master of the world. The dialectician, however, believes that the contradictions of life will be reconciled through dialectical processes inherent in history. Positivism, in turn, argues that it is the unfettered action of man that leads to the goal immediately ahead. The Marxist dialectician argues that the solution lies embedded in the natural order of things, the practical side of which is the dialectical game. For the Marxist, the answer lies in the origin, whereas for the positivist the answer lies in a future that one can never pin down.

As a young student, Karl Marx goes to Berlin, where he joins the circle of younger Hegelians and develops Hegel's earlier social criticism. Hegel harks back to Anaxagoras as the classical model, with his teachings of an original, spiritual, and dynamic energy: *nous.* Hegel argues that the real is the spiritual and that in his worldly, sensual life, man is "alienated" from this spiritual reality. But Marx, more radically than anyone else among the young Hegelians, applies an intellectual idea that is replete with revolutionary implications: the real is the material, the palpable, and man is an integral part of the material world.

Unlike the Milesian philosophers, Marx does not bother to ask what is the fundamental element of the material world. The essential issue for him is that the world, the palpable order, exists; and he takes it for granted that life is inherent in the material world. Like Anaximenes and other materialists, Marx takes *hylozoism* as a point of departure. Matter forms a unity, and life is sensual per se. Life is an energy inherent in matter and, unlike other living beings, man is a dynamic factor of power in life.

Marx adopts David Ricardo's theory of value for his scientific system; he modifies it with his own theory of value and, further, with a completely new philosophy of history. Marxism is not a utopian blueprint for spiritual and moral renovation in the spirit of a Lamenais or of a Leroux; it is conceived rather as a description of the actual condition of the world, and why and how the world must be changed, as prescribed from the perspective of Marx's philosophy of history. This change shall be effected through dialectics. According to Hegel, the alienated material world is characterized by restless activity and by the inescapable conflicts and struggles among men resulting from this hyperactivity. But this human activity in the material world is the indispensable source of dialectical change through which the Spirit will be the ultimate victor. According to Marx, these same conditions rule the material world. Men as individuals and collectively in social classes are involved in mutual strife. On a more developed level, these mutual conflicts take the form of class struggle, which characterizes society, "sometimes openly, sometimes in a hidden way." During these battles and through them, the struggling armies of social classes not only become more organized but also more conscious of their genuine interests, as the Marxist jargon has it. The struggle and the growing consciousness of its deeper significance merge in time into a dialectical unity.

According to the rules of Marxist dialectic, the violent conflict between a ruling social class and the antagonistic inferior class that has been formed under the spell of the ruling class inexorably leads to the annihilation of the ruling group and the victory of the oppressed. What we now witness, Marx declares, is the "ultimate struggle"; for after the proletariat, there will be no other social class to oppress. The bourgeois class is doomed to ruin and annihilation because, as Marx observes, "the bourgeois conditions of production are the last antagonistic form of the social process of production." Dialectical materialism excludes every form of reconciliation between rulers and oppressed. The modified Marxism of the so-called reformers, which attempts through deals and arrangements — above all, in parliamentary form — to achieve a peaceful transformation of capitalism to a socialistic order of things, true believers brand as mere fraud and treachery.

By means of his scientific economic theory and his so-called dialectical materialism, which constitutes his philosophy of history, Marx has managed to give his system of thought a unity that does not demand much justification. Marxism becomes a closed system, penetrated and carried forward by the dialectical movements of history. This self-movement of historical dialectics is not blind, however; it aims at a precise goal. It is teleological. Marx, too, gives us a pseudo-metaphysical system, but he seeks to disguise it by substituting another deity for that of his master, Hegel — namely, sensual self-centeredness. Marx opposes his materialism to Hegelian idealism, thereby giving the impression of having returned to reality; but of course this return is a delusion. For even if we grant that the internal wars of the senses constitute the "motor" that sets the historical struggle in motion, this struggle does not determine the goals that are established on the various dialectical levels, the principal one of which is the annihilation by revolutionary means of the dominant class. For Marx as for Hegel, the vital force is the "goddess" of history, the very teleology that is inherent in the system of dialectics. Just as liberalism presupposes that individuals shall be able to retain their potential for action in order to guarantee progress, Marxism — in its realm of fancy — presupposes that this dialectic of history is an expression of the indomitable proletarian struggle to conquer the dominant class and to bring about the revolutionary change that, it is held, thus completes the historical mission of dialectical materialism.

In a sense, Marxism leads a life of its own, forming a closed system. Descartes had formulated the classical form of the subject-object relationship of profane life. Man as subject, *res cogitans,* looks out on the realm perceived by the senses, the objective order, *res extensa.* German romanticism reached its peak with Hegel, in whose thought dialectical idealism revokes its own duality. In this respect, as in so many others, Marx is faithful to his master. In his so-called Feuerbach theses, he rejects every attempt to objectify reality or to place himself outside of it, so to speak, so as to critically regard it. All ontological and "Scholastical" reflections are put aside. As a radically sensual being, man forms a dialectical unity with his own surrounding reality. *Der vergesellschaftete Mensch,* social man, has no individual self that lives outside of the sensory order, no self that speculates and "objectifies" the world in which mere sensual man, as Marx puts it, produces and reproduces himself and his world, while forming a closed, dialectical unity.

In the dialectical process that evolves in history, every

period terminates in a crisis, a turning point; or, in our own time, in a revolution. Marx emphasizes the importance of the end of feudalism brought about through the French Revolution. In this process he also includes the subsequent conflict between the bourgeoisie and the proletariat. Thus we may conclude that Marxism rests on three foundations: German philosophy, that is, Hegelian dialectics; classical English political economy, primarily the value theory of David Ricardo; and French Revolutionary usages, especially the Jacobin heritage developed and transmitted to the socialist intelligentsia primarily through Blanquism.

By these means Marxism gets its specific structure and appears as a systematic teaching. Marx regards the world in which he lives through this closed system of doctrine, and through this system he makes his observations and prognoses. In this we meet a side of Karl Marx that has puzzled and seduced many observers. Marx's Hegelian pseudo-metaphysics does not stop the development in him of a certain clear-sightedness, nor does it stop him from undertaking a sharp analysis of social reality, which strongly and for the better sets him apart from his contemporaries. He does make awful historical miscalculations — for instance, in 1847, when he argues that the great hour of the proletariat is imminent; but, incontestably, he also perceives the conflicts, actual and latent, which no welfare policies or social reforms can eliminate from the world. Above all, Marx makes prognoses for industrial and capitalistic development with remarkably lucid foresight, particularly so as his life ended when little more than embryonic tendencies of the new industrial society could be observed.

This is Marxism as a structural theory of society, with all of its theoretical elements of political economy and philosophy of history in place. This is the architectural form, so to speak, in which we usually encounter Marxism and through which we perceive its polemical posture. But this is only the outer, "exoteric" side of Marxism. As a doctrinal system, Marxism also has its inner and "esoteric" lineaments; and Marxist "esoterism" is essentially linked with its doctrine of man.

Marxism is usually described as a social determinism in which the single individual becomes an actor in the larger drama, a dependent cog in a huge, self-sufficient machine. This notion is inadequate, however, because Marxism not only is a macrocosmic view of historical events and processes, it also includes a view of the individual as a living organism and a dynamic source of power.

The basis of the individual's place in the Marxist system is an epistemology, a theory of knowledge. For Hegel, thought and its object are one; the real is that which is being thought. This is as if to say that thought thinks itself. This idea can be traced back to one of the founders of the Eleatic school of philosophy, Parmenides. Karl Marx takes over this idea, but as a materialist, he understands palpable reality, or praxis, as the primary reality of which thinking forms but a part. For Marx, reality is not the object in the acts of perceiving and thinking of the individual, because man also is wholly in the empirical world. This does not mean, however, that man becomes only a dependent particle of matter. On the contrary, through his position in the material world man now becomes the dominant force in the unfolding of history. Man and matter, thought and its object, man and the world: all become one.

Descartes is thereby overcome intellectually; and like Hegel, Marx proclaims an intellectual monism. In Marx, however, not the Spirit but the empirical, sensual world is the reality. But this world is not wholly lifeless matter; no, the Greek thinker Anaximenes, for example, held that life extends to matter. Marx incorporates this hylozoism into his system. And in the closed order that Marx conceives, man is both a product of the flux of life and a bearer of this flux. Where, then, is the true nature of man to be found? There is no abstract, definable nature, no human spirit, no "soul," because man is one with empirical, palpable reality itself. Man is therefore essentially an active, concrete being. His life is *praktische menschlich-sinnliche Tätigkeit* — practical, human sensory activity. Man is affected by and affects the world in which he lives. All spiritual activity has its basis in sensory reality, and nothing exists above this reality.

In his *Thesen über Feuerbach,* Marx presents us with his ontological view of man; and in *Die Deutsche Ideologie,* which he wrote with Friedrich Engels, we get the whole picture of social anthropology and social history according to Marxism. When Marx says that man is *das Ensemble der gesellschaftlichen Verhältnisse,* the ensemble of social conditions, this does not mean that he lives only according to the inflexible laws of the material world. On the contrary, man has a unique position separating him from all other living beings. This unique role, according to Marx, consists in the fact that man produces his own means of nutrition. This places him above the level of animals because he creates, "produces," his own life. Man is a producer — and this is one of the key words of the whole Marxist system.

Man must refine nature in order to collect his food. But the very modes in which this productive work proceeds — differing on different levels of development — are what form man's life. It is through his practical and productive life, in his practical process of development, the sensory processes of life, that man is being created and made aware of reality. The notion that ethical, moral, cultural, and religious forces could possess a vitality and role of their own — these are only so many idle imaginings, according to Marx; and the various ideological systems are but echoes and reflexes of the *Lebensprozess,* this

103

life-process. Consciousness does not determine life; life determines consciousness. All is reduced to a biological, sensory, social process of becoming. Marx says farewell to empirical sensuality, to philosophical rationalism, to positivism, and to philosophical idealism — especially the German variety.

The basis of human life is that which is necessary to preserve life. But as soon as elementary needs have been met, new needs present themselves. This is where human history begins: *diese Erzeugung neuer Bedurfnisse ist die erste geschichtliche Tat* — this generation of new needs is the first historical act. The notion of endless human needs is one of the most important postulates of Marxism; and here Marx bows without reservation to the idea of progress. But another determining factor arises in historical development: procreation. This forms the first social bond, the family; and sexual procreation leads to more and more highly developed social conditions. The family is the productive unit from which social interaction in an extended sense can develop.

The productive task in life is thus twofold. Man is a biological being, a *Naturwesen,* with the primary task of preserving his own life and of generating new life through human sexuality. At the same time, man becomes a social being through sensory interaction with the elements of the material world. By means of this dual role man becomes a central, dynamic force in the dialectical drama of life. Here social conflicts arise and grow, to become the drama of history. Through and in these struggles, man becomes more and more conscious of the significance of these conflicts. Finally, the working class becomes conscious of its "historical task," to such an extent that it can finally break its bonds.

But the road to this goal is painful; and here we are brought into Marxian "esoterism." The relationship of the proletarian to his capitalist master is not only an external systemic conflict;

it is also an inner drama, the so-called "alienation." For Hegel, the Spirit is the real, and the world is an external fact; and it is in this divided, unfriendly world that men live, in the midst of their *Entfremdung* and *Entäusserung* (alienation and relinquishment). Marx borrows these two concepts from Hegel, but of course he gives them a different and entirely materialistic interpretation. In the capitalist system, the proletarian is deprived of his position as producer because he must sell his labor, which becomes little more than a commodity. As is the case with his labor, he personally becomes a commodity and is subject to disposition at the hands of his capitalist masters. This is a catastrophe, for the worker now stands as an alien confronting his life of labor. He is deprived of that which makes him a man — the power to produce. Marx denominates this double tragedy, *verlust und Knechtschaft* (loss and slavery), with the twin names *Entfremdung und Entäusserung*.

The labor of the proletarian is a commodity; the worker is forced to sell himself like a commodity in order to survive. He is outside, *entfremdet*; and he is deprived of his true humanity as a producer, *entäussert*. This maiming, this double tragedy, makes the proletarian an irreconcilable enemy of the capitalist economy. No reconciliation is possible. Only the annihilation of the capitalist system by means of nationalization can restore truly human conditions. Man then becomes a producer and is liberated.

To be human is to be productive, producing, creating; *denn was ist als Leben anders als Tätigkeit?* What is life other than activity? At this point, we reach the very center of Marx's view of man; and this is also the cardinal point of the whole conflict, the fact that (according to Marx) capitalism humiliates the proletariat. This humiliation can be overcome only through a dialectical process, the "ultimate battle." Marx adds a third category to this double alienation, to the *Entfremdung der Sache* (alienation of matter) and the *Selbstentfremdung* (alienation of self). Man belongs to a higher unity, his own species. Man is a creative being, according to Marx, and also a *Gattungswesen,* a collective being, a collective personality. This means two things: On the one hand, in purely objective fashion, man as an individual acts on his ambience, his surrounding reality; on the other hand, man is himself a part of this ambience. He is a cosmic *Gattungswesen,* that is, part of life as totality. Man is both an individual and a universal being.

These latter statements must be further qualified. Animals use nature only for their living; but man's encounter with nature is both theoretical and exploratory. It is partly a practical relationship, exploring and exploiting; and, as Marx notes, partly aesthetic as well. Marx's master, Hegel, taught that thought and the object of thought are identical, one and the same; and Marx borrows this position, but with certain underlying assumptions relative to the sensory order. For him, human consciousness and thought, just as aesthetic experience, form a continuum with the world in which man lives. In a similar manner, man is related to palpable nature: *Die Natur ist sein Leib, mit dem er in beständigem Prozess bleiben muss* (nature is his body to which he is linked in a necessary, continuous process). This is because *der Mensch ist ein Teil der Natur,* man is a part of nature, according to Marx's so-called Paris manuscripts of 1844.

The Marxist term *Gattungswesen* means only that man is a cosmic being, entirely one with the material order and with nature. This opens an abyss between the Marxist cosmos and the atomistic order of liberalism that, in its collective aspect, offers community only as the sum of individual lives. Nothing would be more fatal, however, than to assume that Marxism denies the individual capacity for conscious action. In contrast to the animal, man is *bewusste Lebensstätigkeit,* conscious life activity. He is a cosmic being and the dynamic center of his cosmos. Noting man's role as the sustaining, creating, reforming force of the cosmos, we come to another equally decisive point in the body of Marxist doctrine: Man is creator, and man is free.

As long as man is conceived as an individual being, Marx tells us, nothing actually separates him from the animal order. Like animals, man seeks to keep himself alive, to lead a "life creating life" (*Leben erzeugendes Leben*). Only when man has become a cosmic *Gattungswesen* can he develop fully as a free, creative being. The world and man thus become one. Man is both *microcosmos* and *macrocosmos*. His work and the ambience in which his work is accomplished become a dialectical unity, a cosmic accord; *sein werktätiges Gattungsleben* (his active work as creative being) is an unbounded production of new reality.

As a creator, man in this context has definitely taken the place of the divine Creator. The origin of the world does not bother Marx. The essential thing is that every transcendent, creative force is denied and man's omnipotence is proclaimed. Only with Marxism does the Kingdom of Man appear in its stark, existential totality; this is because man, his work, and the natural order in which his work is accomplished now constitute a dialectical unity, a cosmic accord. And in this, his pseudo-divine position, man is also free — free in an absolute sense. This is where alienation enters; alienation means not only that man is separated from the means of production and is deprived from the fruits of his labor. He is also deprived from what may be called his cosmic affinity, the unity between man and the cosmos. This is the culmination of the alienation drama — or better, perhaps, its nadir. The alienated worker is thrown back into an individual state of life, to an animal stage. Mutilated as a man, deprived of that which makes him a real human being — cosmic, universal, creative, and free, he has also lost that which constitutes the human spirit, *Entäusserung;*

and at the same time he has become a stranger to his own true nature (*Entfremdung*).

Alienation is the fatal catastrophe in man's life because he becomes a stranger not only to his own body, his work, and his position as creator, he is a stranger also to nature, to the cosmos — indeed, to all that belongs to his rightful human life. One vital effect of this concerns his bonds with his fellow human beings. He is both cosmic and universal, a natural being and a citizen in a universal brotherhood. Alienation is a catastrophe that takes away his human and social community. Henceforth, the world is rent asunder.

In the speculations of Karl Marx, we find not only a sensory being with material interests, a *homo oeconomicus;* ultimately, we have an "eternal" and an "absolute" being. We are told that evil in the world stems from alienation. Alienation means that some men acquire power over other men, enslaving, plundering, exploiting them. Among other things, this occasions the rise of private property. But the Marxist solution does not concern private property in the first instance, because this is viewed as the result of alienation. And it is alienation and "wage slavery," not private property, that deprives man and cosmos, indeed the entire universe, of their deepest and most primordial significance. In other words, there is a "paradisal" original order of things to which liberated man must finally return. In this paradise is to be found the universal idea of peace — peace that may come as soon as man again becomes the cosmic *Gattungswesen* that he once was.

This is not the place for a systematic critique of the Marxist body of doctrine; for this, I may refer the interested reader to my *Myt i verkligheten* (Myth in Reality) of 1977. Instead I shall offer a few reflections on the question of why Marxism became the teaching that for so long dominated the entire socialist camp, and why ultimately it failed.

When the young Karl Marx came to Paris in 1843, he was unknown. He did not bring with him any finished body of socialist doctrine. Rather, he encountered a plethora of highly elaborated socialist systems, with learned and cunning defenders and large followings. These systems tended to have certain common characteristic features: a static view of society and an often baroque system of social institutions and themes. What these utopian theorists offered was a world of speculation, of ideal states of affairs.

Karl Marx, by contrast, has two points of departure. First, he offers an analysis that he claims is scientific. He borrows heavily from the British school of political economy with its theory of value, to which Marx adds the notion of surplus value. In this way he gives his teaching a scientific basis — to which he eagerly invites attention. At the same time, he makes striking prognoses of capitalist and industrial development, prognoses that are all the more remarkable in that Marx was familiar only with the initial phases of these developments.

The second point of departure for Marx is no less significant. While other socialists, utopians for the most part, describe static, "ideal" systems, Marx thinks in a dynamic fashion. He gives the world a doctrine that, in the form of Hegelian dialectical philosophy of history, presents a picture of how the world changes and how it must change — irrespective of how men think.

The new industrial system, the machine age with its mechanization of life, the unhealthy factories, Blake's "dark Satanic mills," the social, moral, and cultural misery that accompany these developments — all of this Marx condemns no less than do so many others of the time. Marx, however, regards these things affirmatively. He is no reformer, no altruist, no author of idealistic or moralistic paradigms. Instead, Marx sheds an apocalyptic light over this misery; he becomes a prophet and guide through the desert of capitalism. Marxism, indeed, is a kind of eschatology, a teaching about ultimate things. Psychologically, the socialists err not only in giving their adherents closed and static models; they also assume that the reformers have a responsibility to change things for the better. In their appeal to the sense of responsibility, these utopian ideas are genuinely constructive; but the posture of responsibility places a heavy burden on the utopians.

Unlike the utopians, Marxism saves us from these petty considerations. The proletariat participates fully in these historical struggles, but this participation does not entail deep responsibility nor positive duties. The results of the liberating battles are known beforehand; they are predetermined. According to Marx, the proletarian must find his place in a higher, historically fixed order. The goal is in place — a gigantic human liberation. As soon as the yoke of alienation has been cast aside, man can return to the "original" and "paradisal" state of things.

Marxism offers a kind of psychological relief in that it does not demand responsibility in any deeper sense. We cannot understand the attraction of Marxism, however, unless we remember that this socialist doctrine has still another strong source of power: namely, hatred. No one else has known how to exploit hatred so effectively as Marx, and his teachings are full of social and political hatred. Terms like reconciliation, forgiveness, or trust do not exist in the Marxist lexicon nor in the world of Marxism. The dialectical struggle is an affair of life or death. It is merciless, and the result of the struggle involves the annihilation of the losing party — as so often attested in the outcomes of the internal quarrels of the communist states. This hatred was sanctioned not only philosophically but morally as well. For Marx as for Hegel, the good, the just, is what actually occurs.

The dramatic change wrought in the world situation by

the collapse of the communist bloc means not only that one of the two superpowers has vanished, but also that Marxism as the guiding doctrine and state philosophy has effectively disappeared, even as it had long since lost all credibility. This doctrine and this state philosophy existed in a kind of ongoing symbiosis; therefore the apparently double breakup was really the demise of one indivisible system. Hard, brutal reality marked *finis* to a human and social absurdity.

How did this come about? First, Marxism was a system of doctrine that purported to include all of society in its purview. In theory, it was a social totality that posited historically necessary and inevitable processes for all human social life on this earth. The Marxist promise was that history had to "realize itself" in a total revolutionary victory of the "world proletariat." This was to be the revolution that not only brought the proletariat to power, but that at the same time effected the liberation of all mankind. This pseudo-metaphysical tableau of history was nothing more than a phantom, a sinister conceit that reflected inadequate nineteenth-century speculations long since outdistanced. At last even the most dedicated communist could no longer believe in it. The fact is that working men all over the world by and large have chosen the more peaceful way of reformism and trade unionism; and these avenues have yielded much·better living conditions for the working classes than those enjoyed by their brothers in the Soviet paradise.

Second, Marxism informed us that when communism would deliver us from the yoke that capitalism has laid on us, then mankind would emerge in its pristine and "paradisal" form, free, strong, and happy. This new "Soviet man" first of all would be manifested as Producer, meaning implicitly that man would replace God: now, man himself would be the Creator. This in turn means — and we speak only of economic matters here — an enormous development of wealth. Marxism

111

says that the meaning of communism is that we shall have no more exploitation, no more oppression; the productive life, the life of labor, proceeds in harmonious, peaceful cooperation. But at the end of the costly Soviet experiment, alas, it became all too evident to countless loyal Soviet citizens that not even the most elementary demands of life were being provided under the Soviet system, and the crisis for this system was at hand.

Third, Marxism proclaimed that the whole of life and existence is a colossal dialectical unity: that the individual and humanity are one; that humanity and society are one; that humanity and nature are one. But this cosmos, this universal community, can be realized only in the communist ordering of things. All prior systems, especially capitalism, have built their power on oppression and have divided humanity through myriad conflicts and class wars. But communism would issue in a supreme dialectical unity as a reality in daily life, in working life, in citizenship, in social relationships, and between different societies and races. Succinctly expressed, communism would bring peace on earth. The new man, Soviet man, would be integrated into the dialectical unity mentioned above; he is integrated with mankind, with society, with Nature. Universal brotherhood arrives; peace on earth means productive labor and the fullness of citizenship. All take part in a new trusteeship in freedom and equality, and live in peace — this is the new and happy world that was promised for mankind after the annihilation of the great menace of capitalism.

As this grotesque chimera neared its term, every sane denizen of the Soviet bloc became aware that at all points the communist system was yielding the contrary to the claims outlined above. It was evident that the Marxist prophets could only have been dealing in fantasies.

Lucifer

The biblical narrative of the Fall of man has an important double aspect. The fruit that the serpent offers to the first human beings is succulent and attractive; the serpent's offer poses the delights of the external and sensory world and excites the merely vegetative and animal aspects of man's nature — it is the appeal of materialism. But the Fall of man also has a deeper meaning; the serpent urges a more excellent promise than mere experience of sensory delights. The Tree of Knowledge offers man insight; his eyes will be opened, and he will be enlarged and leave behind his state of confident innocence. He will be given an intellectual capacity; he will become "like God."

The serpent's seduction, therefore, has a double meaning. He will show man the route to unreflecting animal lust, to a sensualism whereby man will become a slave to materialism. But something far more dangerous is added to this: man repudiates the fidelity that he owes to God and gives himself up to the greatest of all sins, *superbia*, spiritual pride. He tries to raise himself up to become the equal of the Creator, "to be like God." This self-idolization by man is Luciferism pure and simple. For to ungoverned sensuality is added a haughty, narcissistic self-deception whereby man falsifies, distorts, and

113

manipulates fundamental constituents of his existence and that of the world: namely, the truth that the world comes from the Creator, that the creature can never himself become God or "like God"; but rather that he, man, has the vocation of vice-regency and trusteeship under the aegis and law of God.

Because of progressive secularization — and the confusion that results from it — the West has been ensnared in a Luciferism that has had disastrous consequences in many areas of Western life, and not least in theology. We encounter Luciferism in varying, fluctuating, and often seductive forms; for example, in the "beautiful" system that we call idealism. Idealism presents itself as an elevated, ennobled form of the best in humanity; and thereby it can be interpreted as a line of argument negating materialism and hedonism. But the incense on the altar of idealism has the function of concealing the fundamental fact that idealism, in its anthropomorphic guise, is a form of humanism and thus of Luciferism. It is not at all in contradiction to materialism and sensualism but, on the contrary, is one of the double aspects of the Fall of man. Idealism is the complement to materialism.

The sensual temptation toward the beautiful but forbidden fruits of the Garden of Eden leads to a seduction less dangerous than the Luciferian promise that man will be "like God." To yield to all things in the sensual world that attract is not intrinsically unpardonable — after all, we live in a world of material and sensible objects. If the disobedience of the first human beings had been limited to the consumption of delicious fruit, correction would have been possible. But to revolt against the Creator, in effect to dethrone him — *quod fieri non potest* — by idolizing oneself, this is a catastrophe and is the deeper aspect of the Fall of man. For Luciferism is much more dangerous than the concupiscence that one feels before the attractions of the material world. Moral decay is never so disastrous as pride, the properly

Luciferian intention. Yielding to concupiscence (and, in the first instance, allowing it to assume unmanageable proportions) is a breaking of norms, a degradation, a degeneration that God can counter and heal with his pardon and grace. Pride is a denial, a negation of the divine order itself, a falsification of revealed truth.

Draped in the shining garment of idealism and humanism, the West has accomplished a manipulation whereby the deepest meaning of the Fall of man is concealed. In the name of idealism and humanism, secularization is legitimized. More and more, Western man is living in a world in which he listens only to his own voice, which begins as the voice of rationalism; and listening to this voice, he is able to refer continuously to the "legitimation" that he believes the idealist and humanist pseudo-spirituality confers on him. In this world, secularization progresses because man can be represented as a higher being, carrying "the eternal" in his breast, conquering all creation, and at last proclaiming himself as universal sovereign.

What we call "Western" attitudes, perspectives, and ways of thinking have their sources in Greek thought, and Greek thought was rationalist, at least in its "classical" form. In Greek thought, we encounter a Luciferian element. The Greek conception of reality, at least in its rationalist posture, excludes transcendence; the perfect is reached through the limited, the finite. Being is the highest category, and the infinite and the eternal are excluded.[1] According to an apocryphal tale, a party of ancient Greeks were on a boat at sea; when one of them maintained that beyond the formal and closed world of received wisdom, there must be something that we are incapable of grasping with our rational faculties, he was thrown overboard.

---

1. It must be noted, however, that this "ontic" aspect of classical Greek thought is far different from and inferior to the genuinely metaphysical ontology of the medieval Scholastics and must not be confused with the latter perspective. — Editor

In the Renaissance, the Luciferian temptation advances on a wave of "liberation," even though we are less conscious of this as a road (albeit a winding road) leading to a further Fall of man. Idealism and humanism, regarded as bearers of spiritual light to a secularized world, are so much stronger in the consciousness of the time. And we must note the fact that advancing secularization has and must have the support of a narcissism that promises "self-realization" under the lodestar of everlasting progress.

The nineteenth century is the culmination of Luciferism, and in that century we see three fields of Luciferian conquest. The first can be compared to a cultivation: the opening and exploitation of a mighty landscape, wherein all forms of humanistic, nonmaterial cultivation are brought together in homage, not to the Creator but rather to constitute a celebration of the "human spirit." Culturalism, indeed, is like a tremendous mirror in which man regards himself and in which, in the name of idealism and humanism, the image in this mirror will always be immaculately pure.

The second field of Luciferian conquest is theology. Pietism, with its intimate and sentimental character, undergoes a displacement in the eighteenth century; its center of gravity shifts from the theocentric to the Christocentric.[2] The theologians of the nineteenth century, with the German Protestant Schleiermacher in the vanguard, transform the Son of Man into an ideal human model, thereby placing physical or sensory experience at the center of religion. Nineteenth-century theology deals less and less with God and more and more with man; the transcendent is progressively replaced by the earthly and

2. That is, a reduction of the Logos to merely human dimensions. Needless to say, such reductionism is heretical — especially if compared to that of the Christology of the Greek Fathers or that of the High Middle Ages. Cf. John 16:7: "It is better for you that I depart"; that is Christ in his humanity. — Editor

horizontal. More and more, religion becomes religiosity: intimacy, brotherhood, welfare, consolation, social and mental therapy. The new theology considers that its first duty is collaboration with secular institutions to offer prescriptions — moral in the first instance — favoring strength and viability, liberty and loftiness. No longer a *scientia sacra*, theology strives blindly to achieve a Luciferian goal and regards itself as a collateral, collaborating element among other social forces. The Spanish philosopher Juan Donoso Cortés harshly remarks: They offer God worship, but they do not obey him.

The third field of Luciferian conquest is science (the natural sciences), that "son of pride" — *le fils de l'orgeuil,* in the expression of Joseph de Maistre. For science, the nineteenth century is the epoch of triumphal progress. Knowledge in the Luciferian dream-world has now assigned itself a double mission: It must, through scientific research, discover the forces that govern the Universe; and, by bringing mankind into conformity with this discovered law, it will assure man a position of omnipotence in the world. It is only a matter of time for this position to be reached, and it is significant that the definitive literary formulation of this view was published by the German zoologist Ernst Haeckel in his popular *Das Welträtsel* (published in English translation in 1899 in London as *The Riddle of the Universe*).[3] Very soon, Professor Haeckel assures us, the last blanks on the map of knowledge will be filled in. Then the great day of Luciferian triumph will arrive.

It is in the last trembling minutes of the nineteenth century that Luciferism believes it can claim victory. The liberalization of the Western world and confidence in rational thinking were

3. In that heyday of scientific triumphalism and in his zeal to advance the cause of evolution, Professor Haeckel saw fit to fabricate evidence in the drawings he prepared for this purpose. "Schematize" was the word he used when this was discovered. — Editor

regarded as guarantees against any possible reversion to former barbarian times. Western secularized man was not at all prepared, therefore, for the bitter Luciferian crisis that would overtake him shortly thereafter.

We must admit that nonmaterial creations, rich emanations of fantasy and of artistic form and elaboration, did give the nineteenth century great aesthetic riches; and it should not surprise us if people of the time were filled with self-esteem. We must understand, however, that in all of this achievement we encounter the last radiations from a spiritual source, a higher, divine wisdom akin to that which everywhere has been given to men throughout the centuries. Already in the early nineteenth century there are clear warning signs: Certain penetrations into the nervous system forebode a coming mental crisis. Ambiguous, *outré* romanticism makes inroads into the human psyche; the music of Richard Wagner, for example, manifests a morbidity in its peristatic, tropistic upheavals. Culturalism, the idolization of cultural pursuits, had promised to bring the human spirit to a higher level, mobilizing "the eternal" in man's breast; but now we begin to see suggestions that this spiritual journey is in fact going in the opposite direction.

Aggiornamento, so widely heralded at the beginning of the Second Vatican Council — *aggiornamento,* the accommodation of theology to a more and more secularized world — does not mean that the City of God is vanquishing Lucifer. It means, on the contrary, that the troops of doubters and deniers are increasing. Nor does it help when muddled and anarchic "theologians," in the name of a distorted brotherly love, preach that they will realize the City of Well-being. Those in the West who are on the side of God have to face the brutal fact of largely losing a whole social class, namely, the industrial proletariat. In one sense, the encyclical *Rerum novarum* of Pope Leo XIII was in vain: the working class opted for socialism.

One of the fundamental assumptions of Luciferian rationalism is that the world is a solid, continuous, law-bound unity, and this unity is the object of human knowledge. This is a mathematical and causal conception, formulated by Newton. But already in the last years of the nineteenth century, physicists began to call into question this picture of the material world; and during the first decades of the new century, the "classical" Newtonian interpretation was no longer considered valid. Modern particle physics and structural investigations into matter provide a description of empirical reality much more like Heracleitus' *panta rei*. And as this incessant flux does not provide solid local and causal connections, we cannot reach conclusive answers by structural analysis. It is not in a "downward" direction that man must seek stable and changeless truth, and even among scientists it is sometimes realized that, conceivably, we have to look inward and upward in this quest. More than one of the great physicists of our time have openly declared that we have to reckon with the possibility of a higher, divine order. Lucifer's power begins to waver.

Man can live indefinitely as consumer of the fruits that the Creator has given him, and he can consume these fruits even when he has forgotten whence they come; he even begins to praise himself, as if he were himself the creator of these goods. But in the beginning of our century we are confronted with the bitter harvest of Luciferism. Let us consider art, where the first indicators are clear and distinct by the turn of the century. In cubism, for example, art is no longer pictorial. Portraits and landscapes are no longer objects for the artist. The aesthetic, creative process is now purely subjective; it must be purified of all external objects and models. Now the artist really is a "creator," as everything comes from an inner process, from which all outward sense is eliminated — and beauty first and foremost. In his famous letter to Émile Bernard in 1904,

Cézanne writes: "We must interpret nature with cylinders, cones and spheres." Beyond time and space and beyond all aesthetic rules, the artist is now creating "his own" reality as a model or as models, using geometric figures among other things. Man as artist puts himself in the place of God, for he declares that he creates *ex nihilo,* from nothing and without models external to himself.

Beauty is now an extinct star. Art becomes aesthetic autism, delivered from every rule or norm. The artist and his product are an aesthetic unity; art is a process of creation, going on only inside of the artist. The artist begins from a *tabula rasa,* a clean slate; there is no model, there are no canons, no aesthetic standards or legitimate attitudes. The artist tells us that what he is originating is a creation in its most profound meaning, and that his production is therefore real per se; this reality is in itself the aesthetic dimension. The artist, as personality, is apotheosized, according to Guillaume Apollinaire. In this sense the aesthetic product is said to be "pure," untainted by any outside influence. Art is real because it is identical with the artist himself; art is true because it springs from the artist's personality.

The aesthetic revolution — for it is a revolution — broke out at the beginning of the twentieth century. If we accept literally what the leading theorist of this revolution, Guillaume Apollinaire, says in his little book *Les Peintres Cubistes,* the essential is that Luciferism is pushed to its utmost consequences. But just as Haeckel's work, *Das Welträsel,* derives its epitaph from a ruined philosophy of natural science, the same is true for the aesthetic revolution. In the apparent moment of triumph, the revolution opens the door to Luciferian destruction. Every rule, every norm, every model, all well-rooted criteria are denied. First and foremost, when beauty is not perceived as an emanation from a divine and archetypal model —

when everything is reduced to the dimensions of the sensual world of man, then this world of unfounded and chaotic impressions and fantasy is very soon emptied of all content and meaning.

The process of destruction whereby the beautiful and the ugly, the good and the bad, have lost their distinction and meaning happens at an accelerating tempo and expands over vast areas. James Joyce's *Ulysses* contains eight hundred pages of senseless monologues and dialogues, senseless in content and in aesthetic significance. The essential as regards this novel is that it destroys everything built up in respect of literary form; and in that destruction of form, the shadow figures we meet in the Joyce novel carry on with their equilibrist nonsense.

Let us consider another domain of art, music. Music is a form of art that acoustically turns the senses toward the heart. Nevertheless, in spite of its freedom from every plastic model, music is bound to time by rhythm; and it is bound to space in its architectonic structure, the linear and vertical tone sequences, melody and harmony. Music formed its major and minor tonality in its meanderings through Europe's cultural life. The musical revolution also occurred at the beginning of the twentieth century with Arnold Schönberg as its first protagonist, but initially it did not entail a break with every form. Atonalism, however, opens the door to the liquidation of what has been traditionally considered Western music. In the ongoing musical revolution, the leap into a world without norms leads to electronic or industrially produced music, which lacks an essential element of traditional music: namely, the overtones.

Another leap forward is in the multifarious "popular" forms of music, wherein we have to listen to an industrial rattle combined with a rhythmic intensification to the extent of sleep-producing monotony, even while it is being elevated acoustically to insupportable levels. In this "popular" and "industrial" form, music has the important function of both stimulating and anesthetizing the listener's nerves and of dulling his higher faculties.

What man as a sensual, biological creature has to offer to art is soon exposed. The paucity, the impoverishing effect of secularization becomes increasingly evident, and it becomes urgent to find new forms for sensory stimulation. The ugly, the distorted, the morbid, the malicious are mobilized; representational art becomes anti-art; the novel becomes anti-novel; musical consonance is replaced by dissonance. The divine source of art, beauty as the heavenly model for all that is beautiful on earth, is denied and forgotten. The beautiful in creation, all that we look on as a reflection of the beauty of heaven, has no place in the "creative process" as it is envisaged by the Luciferian artists.

When the divine is totally denied, the ineluctable consequence is that there is nothing else to take its place but the spirit of negation, the satanic. And this is what we must now face up to. Anti-art, anti-novel, anti-music — all have sensual stimulation as their aim, the double purpose being to further weaken vitality and to still anxiety. In these stimuli, in these encounters with the ugly, the distorted, the morbid, the satanic is lurking. The cult of sexuality, for example, can be presented as a hymn to life; but we need to be aware that the biological sex function can become an act of aggression and thereby deeply linked with violence. Moralists the world over lament the explosion of promiscuous sex and violence; but this is more than a moral problem, for the two are interconnected and can easily be engaged as servants of the satanic. "Rock" music, for example, has the dual function of evoking and stilling tensions, and it can simultaneously lead to devil worship.

The Luciferian lies along the road to the satanic. Secularized man proclaims himself as light-bearer; instead, he is prisoner of the Lord of Darkness. Here the Luciferian "progress" loses its sure sign of victory. Science, for example, faces a positivistic crisis; it cannot offer the Archimedian point where we can place our foot and move the world. And in its final stages, culturalism mobilizes a host of functionaries, administrators, and advisors under the banner of UNESCO to legitimize us as cultural beings. But the muse has departed, for reality speaks another language. When the inward, spiritual Light is denied, man is no longer disposed to a vision of God's revealed beauty as reflected in creation and as constituting the genuine source of all cultural creation.

The Luciferian process has an inner logic. Power is not sought in an upward direction; on the contrary, the road leads downhill, and along this road are many telltale signs. One of these is widespread mental disharmony. The Luciferian promise is to produce a free, happy, strong, and harmonious man. Instead we encounter neurosis as mass phenomena. Never before has there been so much talk of "healing," never before so many practitioners of the healing arts. How could it be otherwise? No one affirms more explicitly the downward direction of attention and consciousness in the modern world than the father of psychoanalysis, Sigmund Freud, who chose as motto for his *Die Traumdeutung* (published in English as *The Interpretation of Dreams*) Virgil's sinister *Flecrete si nequeo superos, acheronta movebo*[4] — if I cannot move the gods, I will stir up hell.

But what of theology? Has not Western theology seen the falsehood of the promises of everlasting progress and of all of the dreams associated with this myopia? I will answer the

---

4. Notably, these words were spoken by Dido in a fit of rage and frustration when she realized she was unable to thwart Aeneas in the accomplishment of his heaven-given vocation. See *The Aeneid*, bk. vii.

question briefly and to the point. Theocracy, the affirmation of God's sovereignty and omnipotence over his creation, has slowly diminished and credence has moved in the direction of an emphasis on the humanity of Jesus Christ. The next step is taken when the anthropocentric is unashamedly proclaimed. One hears less and less that the Creator will at some point take back his own creation. Rather, it is widely believed and proclaimed that existentially the world is everlasting and that within this context man must concentrate his powers on achieving a terrestrial and social paradise — notwithstanding mounting evidence that man's best efforts are having precisely the contrary effect. What Platonism taught us — that creation is both fontal from and inflowing to the Sovereign Good — is now forgotten. Two pagan thinkers, the Germans Karl Marx and Martin Heidegger, promise that this world will never have to answer to the Lord. Theology, more and more defenseless vis-à-vis these philosophers and others like them, is a virtual prisoner in a hardened Luciferian grasp.

Fundamental for an understanding of our situation is to be conscious of the fact that existentialism, especially as formulated by Heidegger, is the definitive philosophical formulation of Luciferism. A higher, transcendent Reality is denied; the highest reality is Being, the "ontic" itself, and on this immovable and inaccessible Being reposes our existence.[5] Every idea of creation is excluded, and in this existential world man lives completely deprived of norms. His life has no profound meaning; he has only to preserve himself as best he may in the fleeting, existential flow, which he does by continuous activity. Man is, as Heidegger says, *entworfen* — dispossessed. The good

---

5. It cannot be overemphasized that the "ontology" of Martin Heidegger is not that of the Judeo-Christian tradition (nor of the Islamic tradition, for that matter), notwithstanding a certain commonality of terms which is itself a continuing source of confusion for the unwary. See n. 2 above. — Editor

and the bad, the true and the false — these notions are of no significance; all proceeds from restless and meaningless human activity. This means, in effect, that man creates his own solipsistic spiritual world.

Marxism belongs to the nineteenth century, to the epoch of closed ideological systems. With its Hegelian dialectic and its materialistic interpretation of history, Marxism was an "orthodoxy," one now quite out of fashion. The Luciferian man-of-today is more and more heterodox; for this reason existentialism has been advanced as a more adequate philosophy, the philosophy of the City of Man. Existentialism is a kind of "laughing gas" for the theological *aggiornamento;* it offers endless possibilities for dissolving orthodox systems and for interpreting them in "new" ways. First and last, existentialist philosophy delivers modernist theologians from the "burden" of transcendence. Heaven is a charming story for little children, but "the man who has come of age" has a "deeper" insight; God is "down here," included in our earthly existence and manifested only in human beings and in human activity. The contention between rationalism and faith can now be ended, for faith has been reduced to sentimentality, if not altogether vanquished.

Marxism was always involved in conflict with Western scientific positivism; and here, too, existentialist philosophy dissolves all conflicts. Culturalism also can enjoy unlimited freedom and possibilities. Surely existentialism is the perfect philosophy for Luciferian man in the late twentieth century. But is Lucifer the victor? The world can be covered in darkness, cathedrals can lie in ruins, people can be thrown into confusion and led astray, the light of the Spirit can be obscured. But the false light-bearer, Lucifer, cannot destroy the Spirit. The Luciferian man of our times confronts a sign of the inner truth, and this sign is guilt.

The great secular promise has always been the same: that man — free, strong, and happy — would deliver himself from the burden of guilt. But always, from the Garden of Eden to our own time, man has striven in vain for this impossible deliverance, as if he could run away from his own shadow. This is what Franz Kafka tells us in his novel *The Trial.* The leading character in the story, Joseph K, an insipid and melancholy bank employee, is accused by a shadowy bureaucratic authority of an undefined crime of which he is ignorant. Imprisoned, he meets the chaplain in the prison chapel. The pastor reminds Joseph K of the fact that the law has not only an outward, imperative order, but also an inward order. Not everyone has understood this, even if they have obeyed the law every day of their lives. We always meet differing opinions about the law, and these can even be contradictory. Who in this world is free, and who is bound? The pastor's answer is that to be bound to the law in one's calling, even if only as a porter, is infinitely more precious than to live "free in the world."

This tale has a profound message as well as a plain and direct pedagogical meaning. Reality has a double dimension, the outward and the inward. Consequently, man lives in a two-sided reality. As creation is an order, a cosmos, God has given us a law that has an inward, invisible force as well one that is external. Even the ordinary servant under the law is superior to the Luciferian hero of liberty, who in his psychic inflation imagines himself to be free in the world — even if this ordinary servant has no profound insight into the Spirit as the inward reality of the law. This is what the prison chaplain tries to tell poor Joseph K, tormented by a guilt the meaning and basis of which he does not understand.

Secularized Western man, incarnated as Joseph K in Kafka's novel, is ignorant of the truth that man has two sources of knowledge, *ratio* and *intellectus,* and that man has within

126

him as it were a fragment, or a reflection, of God's infinitely precious immortal Spirit, and therefore he has a soul. *Duo sunt in homine,* there are two in man — this was a maxim of sacred anthropology in the West until the Renaissance. Within the heart of man resides a spiritual light, and he has intellectual knowledge, an intuitive knowledge of divine Reality. Joseph K cannot understand that he can disavow his presumed Luciferian liberty and freedom from guilt. When therefore a court functionary informs him that he must stand trial, he declares that he does not know the law on which the charge against him is based and he insists that he is innocent. But the court servant points out that if he says he is innocent, then there must be a law confirming this innocence. And when Joseph K insists that he is a free man, the functionary says that there must also exist an absence of freedom.

The Luciferian man believes that he has delivered himself from all guilt and judgment, that he is capable of living strong and free in his jovial heathendom. But the guilty man has intrinsic feelings toward his Creator that he can neither throw off nor escape. He does not understand that creation has a double meaning. First, all creation is an outpouring stream of the divine goodness, and we cannot repay all that we are given of this goodness no matter how many sacrifices we may offer. God's love, his beneficence, is greater than the sum of all human striving; and therefore we are always in debt to our Creator. Second, creation is a cosmos, an order, a divine law that determines the nature of things. If we run counter to this law, it is inevitably to our injury and we are guilty before our Creator. This guilt is twofold: It denies God's love and it denies the right order of God's creation, of which we are part.

Guilt is an existential fact that we have no choice but to acknowledge and accept. We know that in the nature of things, we cannot make recompense; but in our inward light, we have the intuition that God places his infinite grace on our side of the scale, thrown out of balance by our guilt. Through his grace our scale is brought back into balance, and we reach a state of gratitude and inward peace. Secularized man, however, believing that he can rid himself of his burden of guilt — as if he could successfully evade his shadow — encounters not grace but the onus of his uneasy conscience. In our time, one of the indicators of this increasingly widespread sense of guilt is the upsurge of neurotic disorders. This is what Kafka's novel tells us, under the symbol of a trial.

A growing feeling of guilt is, then, one of the many signs of the inward crisis in the City of Man. The helplessness of Western theology is often expressed in essays that seek to justify it as a psychotherapeutic institution, instead of telling the truth about God, his nature, his work, and what is required of us. But God's spirit lives, even in the midst of a fallen world, and even if it is denied, concealed, and forgotten. Amid Luciferian confusion, amid a growing burden of guilt, beyond a ruinous Western theology, every day man can meet God.

Man's encounter with God is an encounter with the holy. We meet God in inward and outward meaning, and this meeting is like a point of crystallization of the holy in earthly life, a manifestation of the uncreated Absolute in the relative and the contingent. We have some experience of the holy when, inwardly quiet, we encounter connatural substance. This meeting place is at the center of man's being: the heart; and the quiet of the heart lends to our soul the character of a mirror in which, with the "eye of the heart," we can see rays of the divine Sun. The restlessness and hyperactivity of the world lead us away from the holy; but in a quietened heart, the door opens that leads to the holy.

Our terrestrial existence is a continuous wandering between dream and reality. Life's contradictions prompt secularized man to seek refuge in dreams, illusions, utopias, ideo-logical castles in the air. In his self-deception, profane man thinks that what he receives in his mental consciousness is the real and the objective; at the same time, he hopes that by his dreams, utopias, ideologies, and so forth, he can change the world and make it better. This self-deception is twofold. What he calls real or objective is only the outermost layer of creation, that which is accessible to sensory observation. And what man hopes to do and to achieve in the world is founded on subjec-tivism: on impressions, dreams, speculations.

Man achieves objectivity only when he goes beyond the limits in which he lives as a sensual ego. In the inner light of our heart we can escape from the labyrinth of existence and, with discipline, effort, and the aid of heaven, become aware of divine Reality. Through objectivity, we can encounter the holy in the world; we can conceive of creation as a gigantic symbol of God's omnipotence; we can distinguish between the real and the illusory. In this objectivity, man is conscious of his own position and limitations, but also of his spiritual possibilities by means of which he can receive God's ineffable grace.

We can encounter the world by means of the holy and through objectivity, but with a third element also: through love, God's love. As Creator, he is generous; and this generosity is love, beneficence. As the Absolute, he has given spirituality to man, a reflection of his eternal Spirit. We were created by the Father, and in the innermost depths of our soul we are immor-tal; in this twofold meaning, we are bound to God. All that we have is from him; all that we have, we have received as an emanation of his love. Therefore, we say that God is love. Therefore, the world, and man in the world, must bear witness to God's love.

The holy is presence, and it is also attraction. We seek the holy because the holy means purity and perfection. Objectivity is presence, but objectivity is also attraction. We seek objectivity because we desire Reality and Truth, not illusions and lies. Love is presence, but love is also attraction. We seek love because we will not be isolated or abandoned. We seek God, the very Source of our being.

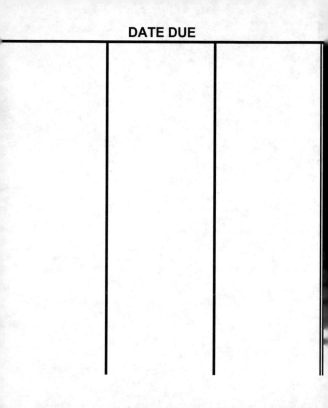

DATE DUE